Tracy Hooper

The
NOW
Hello

Also by Tracy Hooper:

The NEW Hello:
What to Say | What to Do in The New World of Work

The NEW Hello:
What to Say | What to Do in The New World of Work
Audiobook Original

The NOW Hello

WHAT TO SAY
WHAT TO DO
IN THE WORLD OF WORK

Remote | Hybrid | In Person

TRACY HOOPER

INDIE BOOKS INTERNATIONAL®

The NOW Hello

**WHAT TO SAY | WHAT TO DO
IN THE WORLD OF WORK**
Remote | Hybrid | In Person

© 2022 Tracy Hooper

All rights reserved. No portion of this book may be reproduced, stored in a retrieval system, or transmitted in any form or by any means—electronic, mechanical, photocopy, recording, scanning, or other—except for brief quotations in critical reviews or articles, without the prior written permission of the publisher.

ISBN: 9798818022475

Editor: Davia Larson

Editing support by Mary Nienow, Cathy McMahen, Michael LaRocca, Henry Hooper, and Margaret Hooper

Cover and Interior Design: Melissa Farr

**www.ConfidenceProject.com
Info@ConfidenceProject.com**

DEDICATION

For Henry, my wonderful husband, whose belief, patience, and love of me has been a steady source of support of The Confidence Project.

For our precious daughters, Margaret, Eleanor, and Kathleen, who grew up practicing these confidence skills at our dinner table and all the times in between and are carrying them forward into the world.

For my bold clients who trust me to help them move from uncomfortable to confident.

To Team Confidence Project who helped make this book happen: Mary Nienow, Davia Larson, Mark LeBlanc, Sarah Garrison, Carrie Tarbell, Mike Tarbell, Barbara Ipsaro, and Henry Hooper.

—ACKNOWLEDGMENTS—

Special thanks to Mary Nienow. At The Confidence Project, Mary is Director of Systems and Strategic Planning. She's a master at those roles. She is also a deep thinker about the confidence topics and the skills I teach. Mary helps me clarify and refine my messages so that people can understand various perspectives. *The NOW Hello* is all the better for Mary's contributions and care.

Additional special thanks to my editor, Davia Larson. Davia is a voracious reader and thorough researcher. She brings new ideas and alternative points of view to explore and expand what it means to be confident. Her editorial oversight makes *The NOW Hello* robust and accessible to the reader.

Heartfelt thanks to the late Dr. Anthony J. Ipsaro, PhD. He was ahead of his time in graciously teaching young people, and later, corporate leaders, skills for clear communication. Today, Dr. Ipsaro's model and teach approach and diversity training lives on through individuals around the world and The Confidence Project.

— TABLE OF CONTENTS —

Foreword		xi
Introduction	The World of Work: Remote | Hybrid | In Person	xv
Chapter 1	Mindset + Skillset	1
Chapter 2	Plan + Practice = The NOW Hello	11
Chapter 3	Impress + Influence	25
Chapter 4	Presence + Posture + Power	47
Chapter 5	Camera Confidence + Connection	57
Chapter 6	Words to LOSE + Words to USE	81
Chapter 7	The NOW Apology	115
Chapter 8	Own Your Name + Honor Others	133
Chapter 9	The NOW Networking	143
Chapter 10	Confident Conversations	181
Chapter 11	The NOW Goodbye	197
Chapter 12	The Hybrid Highway	215
Conclusion		237
Appendix: Magic Words and Kick Starter Questions		*241*
Endnotes		*251*

FOREWORD

April 2022

There would be no Confidence Project without my parents, Barbara Ipsaro and Vince Bagli. They had six children: Libby, Tracy, Tom, Meg, Missy, and Vince, Jr.

My mother loved being a mom. Our house was busy, but thanks to her, it was an organized, calm, and loving home. Ours was the place where the neighborhood kids gathered to play, inside and out. At dinner time, there was often an extra seat at the table for a friend or our grandparents. Nona on Tuesday nights; Bery and Papa on Sundays. It was at the dinner table and all the times in between that our parents taught us fundamental skills for life.

Every night, just by sitting down and talking together, we practiced how to have a conversation. Through our parents' example, we learned how to listen and speak up, be curious and ask questions. We learned how to welcome somebody into the conversation and how to have difficult ones with respect for the other person.

Our parents knew that if we could present ourselves well, speak up, listen to understand, and treat people with civility, we would be able to navigate life with confidence.

Even when Mom returned to college, graduated, and started her career in counseling, our house was still the hub of hospitality. Our friends trusted Mom because she was truly interested in them.

Our father, Vince, had a stellar career. Dad was a sportscaster in Baltimore, Maryland, for nearly 50 years. His journalism career spanned print, radio, and television, and the sports desk at WBAL-TV was his home. When he was on TV, we kids thought our father had the coolest job: going to ballgames and interviewing famous athletes.

Anywhere we went in our hometown, people would recognize Vince Bagli. "Hey, Vince. Who's gonna win the Orioles game on Sunday?" Dad would smile and say, "Hi. How ya doin'? What's *your* name?" He would easily connect with people that way. Because the exchange became about *them*. No matter the interaction; it could be with the guy hawking beer and popcorn in the stands, the usher, the ball girl, a famous athlete, politician, or movie star, Dad treated everyone the same.

FOREWORD

Without naming it, both of our parents modeled how to treat everyone as if they are the most important person in the room.

In 2014, I started The Confidence Project. From the beginning, my mission has been to teach people how to treat everyone as if they are the most important person in the room. Next to raising our three daughters with my husband, Henry, it's the best job I've ever had.

Thanks to Barbara Ipsaro and Vince Bagli and the other significant elders in our family's life, here's *The NOW Hello*. I could have titled it, *Life Lessons from Our Parents!*

Our dad passed away on October 6, 2020, of old age. He was 93. Our mother is still the strong, elegant, curious, 89-year-old matriarch, modeling to my brothers and sisters, our families, and people everywhere how to treat everyone as if they are the most important person in the room.

Because you are.

Thank you, Mom and Dad, for your life lessons.

INTRODUCTION

The World of Work:
Remote | Hybrid | In Person

It happened for the first time in June 2020, then *again* in March 2021, then *again* in February 2022. I looked at my husband, Henry, and said, "I'm so glad it's *Thursday*." He chuckled. "Tracy, it's *Tuesday*."

"What?"

"Yeah, today is Tuesday!"

Can you relate?

For more than two years, the days, weeks, and even the seasons seemed to get jumbled. Time became amorphous. And for many people, confidence became a precious commodity as we were all trying to figure out what to say and what to do in the new world of work . . . and life. Even with the shock of the pandemic, however, I believed then and now, that confidence can be learned. Yes, there is a part of confidence that's in our genes—in the personality we were born with. The rest comes from taking action.

Take action. Make mistakes. Adjust. Refine. Repeat, over and over.

Today, the world is re-opening. Mask requirements are fewer, and many people are returning to the office. Will it last? Will I eventually know what day of the week it is? It's too soon to know!

What we do know are the massive changes we all experienced when the pandemic turned the world upside down. In January 2021, to address those new and confusing issues, I published ***The NEW Hello: What to Say | What to Do in The New World of Work***. Since then, many of my clients have asked me to write about the ever-changing NOW. What's the confidence playbook NOW? Well, here it is. ***The NOW Hello: What to Say | What to Do in the World of Work: Remote | Hybrid | In Person.***

In each chapter, you'll find new skills and techniques to support your continued remote, hybrid or return-to-office work. You'll find language to use in your everyday interactions to assert yourself, put you and others at ease, and bolster your confidence. And throughout, you'll find Pro Tips for you to use and share with your team and others in your world.

Practice the skills and techniques like you're building a muscle. Before long, they will become second nature. Over time, your practice will lead to a natural way of being that will lower your anxiety. And then, no matter what your personality type, you'll learn to trust yourself and be confident wherever you are: in the board room, a conference room, a virtual room, or even in an elevator.

The NOW Hello also provides evergreen, interpersonal skills and techniques for business. Each one will help you elevate your personal and professional presence and feel calm in all kinds of situations. You can use *The NOW Hello* in every area of your life . . . for the rest of your life. Let's get started!

All the best,
Tracy

CHAPTER 1

Mindset + Skillset

Suddenly, in March 2020, almost everyone who worked in an office was sent home to quarantine. Overnight, WFH (Work From Home) became the acronym of the year. Homes became offices, kitchen tables became desks, and Zoom became a noun and a verb.

In early 2021, after the rollout of highly effective vaccines, cities began to awaken; businesses started to open up. So did schools, restaurants, and theaters. As most of us began to breathe a collective sigh of relief, Delta descended. The variant took hold across large swaths of the country and world and re-awakened our fears. Our lives were upended again along with business plans and reopening timelines. Health experts cautioned that Delta's cousins may come along. They have. Enter Omicron. And since then, other variants of variants.

Officials are convinced that COVID-19 is evolving from pandemic to endemic, meaning, like other viruses, we have to live with it. We also have to live with knowing that there are more surprises ahead in every part of our lives.

As the unsettled questions of WFA (Work from Anywhere) vs. WFH (Work from Home) vs. RTO (Return to Office) vs. Hybrid Work continue to be debated and tested in real time, my clients are still asking: How can I reconnect and interact with prospects, clients, vendors, colleagues, my boss, or leaders with confidence? The larger thoughts behind this are, what best practices can everyone follow to stay safe, sane, and productive? How do I grow my career, cultivate new opportunities, build meaningful relationships, and have a sense of well-being with continued disruptions in every business, every industry, and essentially, every part of our lives?

We humans are social creatures. We thrive on connecting with each other. But how do we maintain our established networks, or better yet, establish new ones, when our old, familiar ways may remain off-and-on for years to come? In-person meetings, big conferences, open-plan offices, water cooler conversations, networking events and off-sites, handshakes, and hugs—will they ever feel normal again? What will become The NOW Hello and The NOW Goodbye that introduce and guide all the conversations and interactions in between? How will our idea of work be reshaped?

Research shows that the pandemic has increased the bonds within teams but weakened the ties across departments.[1]

Collaboration often suffers when we only interact online. Workers say they feel increasingly burned out.[2] Those who work from home worry that they're being sidelined by those who are willing and able to return to the office.[3] More than 40% of workers are considering a job change, but how do you know whether to stay put or move on?[4] For those who have moved on, a part of the Great Resignation, what's their game plan?[5] Perhaps they are a part of a Great Reshuffling, leaving their jobs for a better one or to start their own business.[6] And no matter where people land, what will be the long-lasting impact on strides taken toward greater diversity, equity, and inclusion?[7]

These are just some of the reasons why many people feel off balance. They want to know how to thrive in The World of Work now. They want to know how to stay productive and valued. They want to help their organizations weather the storm as they look for opportunities to advance their own careers. Plus, now they've acquired a taste for flexibility and autonomy, and a majority are saying, "I want more of that." Finally, people are shouting from the rooftops, "There's more to life than work." As one of my clients who's a senior executive told me, "I'm not interested in a work-life balance. I want a life balance . . . Full Stop. A life that is meaningful and joyful. And I wanna have fun!"

There is no returning to the way things were. Or even the "new normal." There is the "new reality." And it's ever-evolving. But that picture isn't clear or consistent. Most everything is in flux, and we are in the messy middle-of-it-all. This new reality is bound to shake our confidence. Even if companies adopt a hybrid approach, some in-office, some WFH, some travel—blending the old and new—it still requires testing out fresh routines, ways of interacting with each other, and work habits. It requires everyone to be mentally, emotionally, and physically prepared to step confidently into new situations and meet the challenges and opportunities of the day.

Definition of The World of Work

The World of Work is the mindset + skillset required to be a resilient, productive, and valued employee, manager, or leader. It requires flexibility, respect, patience, and empathy for yourself and others. It also requires you to toggle from in-person to virtual interactions with ease. Managers and leaders have the additional responsibility to discover new ways to help their organizations grow and thrive while supporting the new demands of their team members. And, all the while, everyone is challenged to have the confidence to be themselves and nurture their own well-being.

More than ever before, doing business in The World of Work now requires a new mindset + a new skillset. The new mindset extends grace to others even when we're frustrated, impatient, or angry. It encourages us to seize new opportunities, even in tough times. It also helps lower our anxiety and stress.

What gets built includes better work relationships, higher performance, and personal satisfaction.

Refining the new skillsets in *The NOW Hello* will give you faith in yourself to move forward with optimism, courage, and confidence. In turn, your colleagues and clients will have a newfound confidence in you. That's when we can *all* do our best work.

Bouncing between conference calls and household chores can mean work life and home life are no longer distinct. David Blustein, a psychology professor at Boston College, notes, "It is often hard to denote when the week is over and the weekend begins, because we are not shifting our location, daily activities or even our outfits." Dr. Blustein adds that "Life is interwoven in a web of endless days and, for many, a lack of clear structure and boundaries."[8]

Leaders tell me that it's still hard to turn off work because they feel as if they need to be fully present for their teams all the time. And team members confide they don't want to be perceived as slackers if they don't respond to calls and emails 24/7.

Set work boundaries to help ease the tensions.

Record a new voicemail message:

"Thanks for calling. My office hours are Monday to Friday, 8-11 a.m. and 1-6 p.m. (time zone). Please leave a message, and I'll call you back. If you need to reach me outside of these hours, please contact my associate, . . . "

Adjust your auto-email response:

"Thanks for your email. My office hours are Monday-Friday, 8-11 a.m. and 1-6 p.m. (time zone). I'll respond as promptly as I can during these hours. If you need to reach me immediately, please contact my associate. . . "

If someone asks you to meet outside of your work hours about a non-urgent matter, use this reply:

"I try not to have meetings after 6 p.m. (time zone). Can we negotiate to meet earlier in the day? I can be available to you between . . . "

Update your OOO
Remember to update your auto Out of Office message. It's unprofessional to see an away message in April that says, "I am OOO from November 23-28 enjoying the Thanksgiving holiday. I will respond to your emails when I return."

As we head safely back into the office, many businesses will continue their WFA policies with virtual meetings, conferences, and interviews. This means even when you're working in the office, you'll often be communicating in person and virtually. That can be a hassle. After weathering Omicron, RTO plans are starting to get the GO button.[9] To keep COVID from spreading at work, companies have pages of protocols. Many are using a combination of vaccine or booster shot mandates. They're also requiring some masking, distancing, and other office procedures that can change as the virus spikes, then retreats. Case counts and mask mandates are still in flux, and reports show that the World Health Organization remains cautious. That's because globally, many countries still have very low vaccination rates. So, there are plenty of opportunities for the virus to continue to mutate and the possibility for new waves of infection.[10]

Still, people are tired of lockdowns, enforced distancing, and other measures that limit their lives. So, it may fall on individuals to take COVID tests and wear masks and be unsocial for a while to keep the virus from spreading if and when it comes back to their region.[11]

Even if we need to wear masks for periods of time or distance to be safe at work, you can grow your confidence and your career. Keep in mind, though, that you and the people you do business with need to feel physically and psychologically safe. Physical safety should be mandated from the top. Companies and leaders must enforce guidelines that keep the virus in check, if variants bring back waves of infection. For people who don't believe in distancing or other ways to keep people safe, we'll discuss ways that you can protect yourself with dignity and confidence.

Psychological safety is an important business concept. The concept of psychological safety was defined by organizational behavioral psychologist Amy Edmondson.[12] It means that everyone in an organization knows they will be accepted, seen, and heard as they are. It doesn't matter where they work or what their job title is. Psychological safety allows people to speak up for themselves and stand up for others. A psychologically safe workplace does what it takes to keep the business thriving while valuing the dignity and worth of every employee even in a fluctuating economy and an uncertain world.

The World of Work now may still feel strange, but there are lots of professionals who have been dealing with similar physical constraints for their entire career. For instance, operating room nurses and doctors have mastered reading each other's eyes with masks on their faces.

While many people are ready to ditch their masks—and have, others aren't there yet. They may want to keep wearing them for any number of personal safety reasons. Either way, this book will teach you how to express yourself with respect for everyone.

As a news reporter, I learned early on what it took to be camera ready and hold the viewer's attention. This was long before I recorded videos from my family room and started leading virtual presentations. I'll teach you insider techniques for camera confidence.

It's important to remember that no matter how long we've been dealing with this pandemic, we are all still learning how to treat one another with civility. We also need to teach others how we want to be treated. That's why, in my definition of The World of Work now, empathy is key. When your plans go sideways—your child makes a cameo on a Teams call, you and your housemate both need to Zoom at 2 p.m., or your pandemic puppy escapes out the front door—take a long, deep breath and downshift into compassion. These days, have empathy for other people. And save some for yourself, too.

The mindset commute

If you work full-time at home and you still miss the mental transition you had between home and office, pre-pandemic, take a "mindset commute." Trade the frustration of traffic and hassles of public transportation for something you enjoy; walk, run, bike, meditate, listen to podcasts, or go to your favorite coffee spot. Take the same amount of time you would normally allow for your former commute. Your "mindset commute" can get you in the right headspace for the day ahead or give you time to unwind when the day is over. Doing activities you like lets your body and mind know that there's a shift coming: "My day's starting or wrapping up."

We will continue to adjust as circumstances change. And they will. They are! Our confidence might be shaken when things don't go as planned, but by adopting this new mindset and practicing these skillsets, you'll be able to manage tough days with resilience, flexibility, and new or renewed confidence.

CHAPTER 2

Plan + Practice = The NOW Hello

> *"Your smile is your logo. Your personality is your business card. How you leave others feeling after having an experience with you becomes your trademark."*
> – Jay Danzie

When COVID vaccines first became available, there were high hopes that they would provide a quick exit from the pandemic. That didn't happen. Instead, we learned that any exit was complicated. Enter the Delta variant, break-through infections, then Omicron, scarce COVID tests, and vaccine hesitancy. Add differing regional responses and pockets of COVID spikes, political polarization, and low vaccination rates (still) across much of the globe. All of these issues mean that there is no quick exit. Our best hope now is to learn to live with COVID long-term.

In the midst of it all, we're *still* trying to figure out how to greet each other and interact with confidence. Many of us fall somewhere between feeling fearful, awkward, or throwing caution to the wind, no matter who we're greeting—co-workers, bosses, vendors, prospects, clients, and even our friends. The pandemic has made us confused, and we wonder, "How are we supposed to be as human beings? What are we supposed to say and do now?"

Why We Miss Close Encounters

Handshakes date back to Neanderthal times. People showed their hands to prove that they weren't holding a weapon. Safety is still one of the major reasons we greet people. Happy hormones are another. When we shake hands, that web-to-web contact, as the inside of our thumbs meet, releases oxytocin. That's the hormone in the brain related to trust and bonding and a whole slew of other positive feelings.

Pre-COVID, a handshake was one of those first impressions that marked how professional you were. In the U.S., unless someone is injured and offers their left hand, a firm grip with your right hand was seen as socially acceptable and professional. A "dead fish handshake" sends the opposite message.

Once, at a business lunch, I introduced myself to a well-known architect who designs bridges. This is a big deal in Portland, Oregon, which is known as "Bridgetown," with twelve unique bridges crossing the city's Willamette River. As we shook hands, the fellow said with surprise, "Wow. You have a really firm handshake—for a woman!" I smiled and said, "Thank you. You have a really firm handshake—for a man!" We both laughed, recognizing the absurdity of his comment. Of course, I have a firm handshake.

Handshakes, hugs, fist bumps, high fives, or la bise (the French kisses on the cheek) are all ways that humans build warmth, intimacy, and trust. It marks the beginning of or reinforces a relationship. Even at a physiological level, there are countless benefits to physical touch, and that's why we yearn to return to the "normal," pleasant hellos and goodbyes.

These days, however, it's not easy. Every day, we're making personal decisions based on risk tolerance, from going into the office (if it's open) to sending kids to school with or without masks to traveling and attending events in the flesh. It's natural to feel "decision fatigue." To relieve the anxiety of *"what do I say and do now?"* decide what makes you comfortable, then Plan + Practice.

I. The NOW Hello Prepares for the Best Leaders

It's your job to set the safety standards and faithfully stick to the protocols that you or your company mandate. Your people can't do their best work when they feel their health is at risk. As a leader, you determine the behavior from the top down. As one executive told me, "If a boss doesn't wear a mask and physically distance, the team won't either. At my company, some key people never believed COVID-19 was a big deal. Others think that once they're vaccinated it's back to pre-pandemic life. So I'm clear to say, 'For the time being, this is what we'll continue with: masks, sanitizers, physical distance. I lead by example. If I get criticized, so be it.'"

Sam is a Confidence Project client and Senior VP at a regional west coast bank. He was preparing for his company's annual board of directors meeting. It was being held in person with everyone required to wear a mask. The problem was, one board member didn't believe in masks and refused to wear one, even when requested.

To pre-empt a potentially uncomfortable and unsafe situation, Sam and I crafted this email to send to all board members:

"We look forward to welcoming you to the annual board meeting on June 22nd. It will be in the large Mountain View Room where we can physically distance. We require masks for anyone who attends, regardless of vaccination status. If you choose not to wear a mask, you are welcome to join the meeting remotely. Please let us know by June 20th so we can send you the video link. If you will be joining us in person, we will have extra masks on hand."

Pre-emptively, Sam also decided he would be the point person to speak to the board member or anyone who arrived maskless. He practiced out loud, "Welcome. It's good to see you again. I hope you're doing well. As you know, we're requiring masks. Here's one for you."

If someone refused to wear a mask Sam was ready, "We've set aside a private conference room here for you to participate remotely."

Every organization needs a plan, even during a late-stage pandemic. There is plenty of state and federal guidance available that is constantly updated as the pandemic, vaccination protocols, and scientific evidence evolves.

Even with office protocols, there are still sticky situations. What happens when you are doing business in person, but outside of the office? Or when invitations for in-person networking events land in your inbox? What about off-site team events that are day-long, overnight, or several days with travel and a hotel stay? Read on.

Managers and Team Members

Countries, states, and companies have different requirements. Do you need proof of vaccination, a rapid test, or quarantine to attend events or return to the office? Individually, we determine our own boundaries, too. Wear a mask or not? Distance? Shake hands, hug, high five? Here's one way to feel confident and prevent an awkward response that can leave you (and others) confused or uneasy. Before you go to a meeting or a coffee with someone new, or attend a conference, trade show, industry, or networking event, develop your Plan, then Practice.

- Plan what you'll do: physical distance, handshake, high five, fist bump, hug. Or not.
- Practice what you'll say ahead of time in the mirror, in your car, on your daily walk.

There is no one-size-fits-all solution.

If you feel safer wearing a mask, start putting it on as you go to greet someone. It's a visual clue that you prefer masks. Most thoughtful people will notice you putting yours on and will put theirs on, as well. Now, neither of you will feel awkward.

II. There is More Than One Good Answer

Hand to Heart, Handshake, or Hug?

So, what can you do if you're not ready for physical greetings like handshakes, hugs, or high fives? Hellos can be verbal, nonverbal, or a combination. What's important is that your words and body language match. Be clear and gracious. Assert your boundaries with a firm and friendly tone. The best way to avoid discomfort is to choose and practice words and actions that feel the safest and most natural for you and stick with them.

To Keep Physical Distance and Mask

If you are still being cautious or are slowly beginning to reconnect in person, there are many ways to greet people with confidence.

- When greeting someone who clearly wants to shake your hand or give you a hug, slightly step back, use your 'I Statements' to express your boundaries, and smile.
  - It's great to see you! I'm waiting a bit longer to shake hands, but it's fun to see you in person!
  - I'm still not shaking hands, but I'm good for an elbow bump!
  - I'm excited for masks to come off, but I'm not there yet.
  - I feel more comfortable at the moment wearing a mask.
  - Masks are optional at our company now, but I'm still wearing mine. You're welcome to not wear one.
  - I'm still wearing my mask, but I'm ok with you not wearing one. Thanks for understanding. It's great to see finally see you in person.

- Raise your eyebrows and nod. Raising your eyebrows is the classic nonverbal cue that says, "I notice you. I'm happy to meet you, and I'm curious about what you have to say."

- Offer a wave, thumbs-up, or tip your imaginary hat. James Taylor tips his cap as a greeting to his audience, a thank you for warm applause, and when leaving the stage after his encore.

- Air hugs from an appropriate distance. Say, "Let's air hug. It's terrific to see you. How are you doing these days?"

- Clasp your own hands, with your thumbs tap your heart, and nod. Smile with your eyes.

- Place both hands over your chest and borrow from the Asian tradition with a slight bow.

- With hands together, palms touching, offer a Namaste.

- Greet people with a big smile. You can even wrap your arms around your own shoulders, hugging yourself as if you are hugging the other person. They'll get the message, "I am hugging you through me."

Regardless of vaccination status or natural immunity, not everyone is fully ready to return to high-density social settings or even small gatherings. If a client or colleague says they've been traveling or getting out and about and you're not comfortable, feel free to say, "I'm glad you're doing well. I'm not ready to shake hands, and I'm still keeping my distance, so let's meet outside or across the table in the conference room."

Additional Distance Options and Mask
Call them on the Phone

"Elle, based on what we've told each other, I'd feel more comfortable if we met by Zoom instead of in person. I hope you understand."

"Stan, how about a Virtual Coffee by Zoom? I'm more comfortable doing that for now."

"Catherine, before we get together, I want you to know that I'm still working from home and mostly with my family. How about you?"

Their response will help you decide how you want to meet them.

Send an Email

"Hi Xhoana, I hope you're doing well this week.

I'm looking forward to seeing you next Tuesday at 1:30 p.m. at my office, 123 NE MLK, Jr. Blvd. I'm still wearing a mask, and I'd appreciate it if you'd wear one, too." Or ". . . and I'd feel comfortable if we both wore one." Or ". . . and it's fine with me if you don't wear one."

Thanks, and see you soon,
Caroline"

Send a Text
"Hi Steve. Looking forward to seeing you tomorrow, October 19 at Peet's Coffee, 1441 NE Broadway. I'll be the person wearing the red, black, and gold mask to match my Maryland Terrapins coffee mug!"

"I Statements" at the Ready

There are ways to let people know in the moment that you want to keep a safe distance without becoming defensive or confrontational. If someone else doesn't seem concerned about safety or protocols and comes in for a handshake and says, "Oh, come on. We can shake hands now." or "Don't worry. I've had COVID, and I'm 100% now" you'll be able to clasp your hands, smile, and confidently say:

- "I'd love to but I'm still being careful. And so far, so good, I've stayed well! Great to see you in real life!" Then, start the conversation.

At the office

- "I'd love to, but let's stick with our company plan to distance for now. Thanks for understanding . . . It feels odd to be back in the office. How's your reentry going?"

- "I wish I could give you a hug, but I'm spending time with my elderly parents, so I'm not hugging these days . . . Tell me, how's your business doing?"

In a narrow hallway

- "I'll wait here. Go right ahead." Add a "go-ahead" open hand gesture and a smile.

- "I'll step back." (to keep distance)

With a new client or a visiting customer

- "As a company, we're still distancing. Thanks for understanding."

- Give a slight wave, then say, "Good to meet you. Our company policy is to distance, for the time being, but I'm glad we can finally meet in person. Come on into the conference room."

- "I'm not shaking hands quite yet, but it's great to finally meet you in real life, not on Zoom!" Then, get right into the conversation.

Are You Ready to Handshake and Hug?

Many people are ready to shake hands and hug. Or they've been doing both all along. Dr. Linsey Marr is an aerosol scientist at Virginia Tech University and a leading expert on airborne disease transmission. She calculates the risk of exposure during a brief hug can be surprisingly low, especially if each of you is fully vaccinated and boosted.[1] With new variants likely to come along, though, it's good to keep updated on CDC guidelines.

If you're comfortable shaking hands, hugging, or leaning in to talk, it's still important to ask your co-worker, client, or new acquaintance what they prefer. Be gracious and nonjudgmental. What's important is to allow others to express their own risk tolerance and for you to honor it.

Example

Joanna, a member of the sales team is ready to shake hands. John, a prospect, is at various points along the spectrum. Here they are in person as they greet before going into a meeting.

Joanna: "John, great to meet you in person. Would you like to shake hands or not? (*Or* should we shake hands?) It's completely up to you."

John: "No, not yet. But I'll elbow bump!"

Joanna: "Great! . . . Come on into the boardroom. There's plenty of space around the table."

Note: Don't dwell. If you respond confidently, so will they.

Pre-Meeting Phone Call

Joanna: "Hi, John. It's Joanna Baruch."

John: "Hi, Joanna. How are you today?"

Joanna: "Doing fine, thanks. Do you have one minute for a question, please?"

John: "Sure."

Joanna: "Before we get together, I want to let you know that I respect your comfort level regarding masking, shaking hands, and distancing. What are you most comfortable with? Any answer is good."

John: "Thanks for asking. I still wear a mask in public, and I'm not comfortable shaking hands, yet. But let's fist bump, or I'm good with Namaste!"
or
John: "I'm wearing a mask for a few more weeks, but I'm fine if you don't wear one."
or
John: "Thanks for asking. I'm totally comfortable shaking hands, and I'm not wearing a mask anymore. There's lots of space here."
or
John: "Masks are optional at our office, so I'm not wearing one."
or
John: Our company doesn't require masks anymore, so you're welcome to take yours off or not wear one. I'm not wearing a mask these days."

Joanna: "Good to know. Thanks. I'm happy to follow your company's safety protocols. See you tomorrow."

All these examples Pre-empt the Awkward.

Mask-Free for You
If you are comfortable mask-free and shaking hands, still respect others and honor their boundaries. If they are

uncomfortable then step back. If they are comfortable shaking hands, shake away! Let them take the lead.

If you want to hug a close colleague or friend, ask for permission first. Remember, add a smile and you're golden! Say,

- "I'm fully vaxxed and boosted and comfortable with hugging. How about you? Either way is fine."
- "Are you hugging?"
- "I got the jab. Are you comfortable with a hug?"
- "I'm hugging again! But it's up to you. Yes and no are both good answers."

If they say, "No," smile and say, "Thanks for telling me." Then offer a warm greeting.

The NOW Hello honors the fact that human beings want to be acknowledged and respected. With or without a mask, a handshake, or hug, if you offer a kind "Hello," people will feel good. It works in person or online. Even with co-workers whom you Zoom with every day, don't forget a simple "Hi, how are you doing today?" It only takes a moment to show that you care about them.

Make your **Plan**, then **Practice**. And be confident that *if* new variants appear, or *if* case counts climb, you can be flexible and adjust your "Hello" to put everyone at ease. We are all truly in this together, facing whatever the future holds and figuring it out one "Hello" at a time!

CHAPTER 3

Impress + Influence

A few years out of college, I was hired at WBOC, a tiny television station on the eastern shore of Maryland, about 120 miles from Washington, DC. When I got there, Bill Jones, the News Director, said, "I know we've hired you to be a reporter, but we'd like you to do the weather for a while."

I stumbled. "Well, ah, I don't know anything about the weather."

"That's OK. The sports guy will teach ya!"

And sure enough, Marty Thorsen, the sports guy, who'd been anchoring weather and sports since the weather guy walked off the set, became my coach!

He gestured towards a map on the wall and said, "OK. Brush up on your geography. Learn the names of the local towns." Then pointing to the corner of the newsroom, "And the weather wire is over there. So, just rip 'n read." Rip 'n read?

On Monday, Marty started coaching me. By Friday, I was "The Weather Girl!" (Yes, that was the title for women weather anchors.) I was terrified, traumatized, and terrible. And it didn't take long before viewers' letters started coming.

> "Miss Bagli,
> "Where the hell did you get that hair? It looks like a nest to put eggs in. Sixty of us at the condo agree. Get a wig."

> "Dear Miss Bagli,
> "Please buy your hair a Valentine! Get it cut, styled, whatever. And what's with all the waves? They make me seasick every time you're on the air."

Finally, I got an "atta girl." A viewer named Eric Bacon wrote to the News Director. "Tell Tracy, it's OK about all the mistakes she's making. She'll learn."

That letter was profound for me because in that moment, even though I had made a lousy first impression with many mistakes on the air, I knew I would get better and more confident with practice.

First impressions, like a welcoming Hello, never change. In person or online, the brain makes assessments in the blink of an eye based on what it sees—face, facial expressions, makeup, hair, posture, grooming, clothing—all with mind-boggling speed.

An article from the Association for Psychological Science reports on a study by Princeton University psychologists who found "that all it takes is a tenth of a second to form an impression of a stranger from their face, and that longer exposures don't significantly alter those impressions."[1] No judgment. That's the way our minds work. In addition, humans have micro-expressions. These are "facial expressions that occur within a fraction of a second," says Dr. Paul Ekman, who's a pioneer in the study of facial expressions. According to Dr. Ekman, everyone has micro-expressions, and they cannot be prevented: "Regardless of culture, language, or personal background, we all share this common form of nonverbal communication."[2]

How fast does the brain move to process facial expressions? Typically, 33 milliseconds![3] The brain goes to work this fast by clueing into micro-cues. Dr. Patricia Kuhl studies micro-cues as a social neuroscientist at the University of Washington in Seattle. Her research shows that the brain picks up on the tiniest of cues that help humans connect with each other.[4]

We crave those interjections like "hmm" and "ah huh," plus small nods, facial movements, active eyebrows, even slightly cocking your head and leaning in show people you're listening to them. That they matter to you. And that builds trust.

But these micro-cues are hard to pick up on video screens. Dr. Kuhl says, "It's all exquisitely tuned. Seconds are an eternity; milliseconds are what matter . . . If you're not actually in the same room as the person you're talking to, making those cues explicit is a first step."[5]

Make a positive first impression and express your good intentions, and that will boost your chances of success; people are more likely to talk with you, listen to you, interview you, hire you, mentor you, promote you, sponsor you, and recommend you. Allowing others to sense your good intentions helps you earn their trust. This is the most important factor in earning the respect of co-workers and your boss and landing business from prospective clients.

It has always been true that your face is your Sphere of Influence. But when three-quarters of our faces are covered by a mask or confined in a square on a screen, it is much harder to make a good first impression or read someone else's face. We're missing those small visual signals that our brains look for to help us decode someone's mood or mindset. So, let's talk about how to make a great impression whether in person wearing a mask or on a video call.

In Person, Wearing a Mask

Though it may seem difficult or impossible to make a good impression without the use of your go-to smile, there are other ways of showing people that you are open, friendly, and confident. You can incorporate small, simple techniques that bring big results.

Doctors, nurses, and other medical professionals train themselves to read people's eyes early on in their careers. Dr. Bruce Bolton, an anesthesiologist in Portland, Oregon, says it becomes automatic. He told me, "I've been wearing a mask for 10-12 hours a day for 30 years. The operating room is our office all day long. We socialize and communicate any range of emotions and stress levels just like other co-workers in a normal office." Dr. Bolton looks for these cues: Upward movement of the face means his colleague is smiling. Squinty eyes indicate they are concerned. Raised eyebrows may mean they have a question for their colleague.

Medical professionals aren't the only people who have to use their eyes to communicate a range of emotions. On the TV show *America's Next Top Model*, supermodel Tyra Banks coined the term *smize* to describe "smiling with your eyes." It is a way of communicating through your eyes while keeping the rest of your face neutral.[6]

Smizing has new meaning when people are masked. Our mouths are covered, but we still want to communicate approachability and warmth. Ms. Banks describes how to smize. "Think of someone you love . . . someone that fills your heart with joy. Now imagine they are standing in front of you. Begin to smile, and not a blank smile that only involves the mouth. Smile with your entire soul. Even though your mouth is covered by a mask, that person on the receiving end will truly feel your kindness through your eyes . . . and they just might smize back at you. The 'synchrosmize.'"7

With or without a mask, active eyebrows can boost your smize. Lift them and look more awake and more approachable. Raised eyebrows are also a nonverbal sign of curiosity. It says to others, "I notice you. I'm listening. Tell me more."

- In most Western cultures when you make eye contact with someone, you make them feel important.

- If it's tricky for you to look someone in the eye, look at the bridge of their nose. It's a great fake!

- Consider taking a picture of yourself, maskless with a smile. Then pin the photo onto your shirt, sweater, or lapel to show people what you look like, mask-free! Some servers in restaurants use this technique, and guests appreciate it.

Making a Good Impression In Person or Online

In person or on the small screen, facial expressions are more important than ever. And there's nothing better than a "Pleasant Resting Face." But that's hard to find in our culture. In print and digital media, we're bombarded with images of people with blank expressions looking disengaged. In some photographs, a distant stare on a model's face seems to say, "I'm hip and unapproachable." Many print ads show the brooding, tough guy lounging in his designer jacket with an expression that I call a "Nasty Resting Face."

And since these images are everywhere, we tend to imitate what we see and can unconsciously wear our own Nasty Resting Face.

Maybe you know someone who suffers from Nasty Resting Face and doesn't know it. My friend, Mark says when he was in college, friends would stop him on campus and ask, "Are you ok? Is everything all right?" "Yeah. Why?" "Because you look mad all the time." Mark said, "I never knew that about myself."

A Pleasant Resting Face is a soft smile, slightly lifted cheeks, engaged eyes, and, at times, raised eyebrows. It's gender-neutral, and it's not a pose. It's an open expression that says to others, "You can feel safe with me. You can trust me. Let's talk."

If you're not sure what your Pleasant Resting Face looks like, check out yourself in the mirror. With kindness, introduce yourself to yourself. Fire your inner critic who spots every blemish or flaw. Instead, hire your inner coach who's happy to meet you. See the natural facial expression that other people see. Then, as you honor your reflection, practice what psychologists call "mirroring." Typically, that happens when you smile at someone, and they smile back. (The 'synchrosmize!') Be that person greeting yourself with a Pleasant Resting Face in the mirror.

On video calls, it's hard to read facial expressions, especially with a group because the screens are small and one-dimensional with people in the old *Hollywood Squares*-style boxes. There isn't the same exchange of person-to-person energy that you feel when you are physically in the same room. During a Confidence Project workshop on Zoom, one person sheepishly admitted, "I never knew I had a Nasty Resting Face until we started constantly Zooming. Now, every time the screen freezes, it catches my worst expressions!" Another person chimed in, "Zoom is like having a mirror follow you around all day long!" We all laughed! Yet another pandemic phenomenon, "Mirror Anxiety."

Sometimes I appreciate seeing my own face. If I notice I have an expression that could be misinterpreted, I can catch myself and switch it up to a more neutral or Pleasant Resting Face.

When you develop a Pleasant Resting Face (or your PR Face!) there is a virtuous cycle spiraling up. As you get better at practicing it, you'll begin to get positive feedback. People may start to talk with you more and listen to you. In turn, you may start to feel better about yourself from the inside out. With time, your Pleasant Resting Face will feel more natural and become more automatic. Like any skill, practice makes progress.

As you wear your Pleasant Resting Face, make your microcues super clear. Practice nodding, lifting your eyebrows, and leaning in. These tiny cues help you to build a deeper connection with others, especially online.

If seeing yourself distracts or bothers you, click on the "Hide Self View" feature on Zoom. Every platform is different. For instance, on Microsoft Teams, you cannot un-see yourself. One client suggests taking a sticky note and placing it on the bottom right-hand corner of your screen so you won't see your face!

In Person or Virtually

Three distractions: Some hiring managers have said that when interviewing people, their top three distractions are people who

1. **Play with their hair.** Fluffing, twisting, and tucking it behind your ears is distracting. And it's not only women. Plenty of men have grown their hair and "pandemic beards." As a senior partner at a large law firm told me, "This beard is new for me. So, I find myself playing with it a lot." Lose that distracting habit.

2. **Adjust their glasses.** When we're nervous or anxious, we can slip into this unconscious habit. Your optometrist

will be happy to adjust your glasses or show you frames that can sit more securely on your nose.

3. Use the Filler word "like." It's overused and often unnecessary. Practice the Power of Pause to catch yourself before automatically saying "like."

If you want to know what distracting habits you may have when speaking, record yourself on your phone or on Teams, Zoom, WhatsApp, or whatever platform you use. You'll quickly notice certain behaviors that you want to change to make a better impression.

Remember: Be patient. A reasonable goal is to lose one distracting habit every 30 days.

> *"Practice isn't the thing you do once you're good. It's the thing you do that makes you good."*
> – MALCOLM GLADWELL

If your face is your Sphere of Influence, then remember the expressions from your eyes and mouth are the Sources of Your Personal Power. Online conversations make it harder to connect, but if you want to make a great first impression, make sure others can see, hear, and understand what you're saying without those unconscious and often annoying distractions.

Helping Hands

When Seth Meyers first left *SNL* to host *Late Night,* he said he didn't know what to do with his arms and hands. He was used to gesturing with his elbows propped up on the *Weekend Update* desk. When he first walked onto the large *Late Night* stage, he gestured wildly and joked, "I looked like someone on a desert island trying to signal for a passing plane."[8]

In Person or Online

Showing your hands is more important than ever. In fact, people who show their hands are rated as more friendly, accessible, and trustworthy.[9] Using your hands with intention will clarify your message and strengthen your connection.

According to psychologists, our hands help communicate our message. When we don't use our hands, we can be perceived as indifferent. These examples illustrate how the positioning of our hands signals our feelings and intentions to others:

- Keeping your hands hidden in your pockets, crossed under your chest, or clasped behind your back makes it hard for people to trust you.

- Finger-pointing is threatening and can be intimidating. Instead, holding your hands open with your palms facing up will signal that you are open and honest.

- Talking with palms down means you know what you are talking about!

- Keeping your palms facing each other with your fingertips touching like a steeple can indicate that you are an expert.

- Grasping your hands in front of you signals you are nervous or tentative.

Touching your face, hair, or neck signals you are unsure. If your hands gravitate to your hair, eyes, mouth, or neck, practice putting them back in your lap, on the armrest, or on your desk.[10]

Record again!

Practice. Record. Review. Practice like an athlete watching their game tape to improve. Press record on Google Meet, Blue Jeans, or the video platform you use and start talking. You may not notice where your hands habitually go until you watch the playback. It can be embarrassing and illuminating.

Remember to Laugh. Nobody's watching except you!

Now that you're aware of what your hand gestures are saying, use them with purpose to deliver the message that you really want your colleagues and clients to remember.

Gesture Library

Without seeing other body language that accompanies and reinforces our words on a video call, our minds need to work overtime. To give everybody's brain a break, use your "Gesture Library."

- **Say:** Welcome everybody.
  Gesture: Arms outstretched, palms open.

- **Say:** I'll cover three points today.
  Gesture: Hold up three fingers.

- **Say:** At the top of the list.
  Gesture: Raise your hand high with your palm facing up.

- **Say:** We value our inclusive culture.
  Gesture: Curve your arms as if you're holding a big ball.

- **Say:** We want to elevate everyone's video conferencing skills.
  Gesture: Simultaneously, lift both hands with palms up.

- **Say:** Josie, let's hear your idea.
  Gesture: Extend your open palm to indicate that you welcome Josie's thoughts.

- **Say:** On one hand. On the other.
  Gesture: Raise one hand with your palm up. Then raise the other hand with palm up.

- **Say:** Here's a small idea that will make a big impact.
  Gesture: Put your thumb and pointer finger close together = small. Arms open to shoulders = big.

- **Say:** One final comment.
  Gesture: Hold up your pointer finger.

Add your own ideas or watch other people's hands to add to your Gesture Library.

Don't Over Gesticulate

As with everything, use common sense. Over gesturing can be as distracting as playing with your hair or tugging on your beard. Use your hands with purpose to help communicate your message with confidence. Then, you won't look like "someone on a desert island trying to signal for a passing plane!"

Consider a Prop Box

Now that my presentations are mostly virtual, I use props to keep the trainings lively and interactive. I hold up newspaper articles and read key lines, magazine photos of Pleasant and Nasty Resting Faces, a microphone, cell phone, coffee mug, and books I recommend. For one exercise, I ask participants to bring a piece of blank paper and a thick marker. They respond to a question by writing their answer on the paper and share it by holding it up to their cameras. This simple activity personalizes the training, helps keep people engaged, and gives me the chance to acknowledge them.

Expand your Gesture Library and Prop Box to match your business culture. This informal but useful visual language improves your clarity and underscores the points you're making. People are more likely to remember and repeat your message, and that builds confidence.

The NOW Dress Code
#WFH

"I haven't put on a pair of hard pants since 2020!" That's how one of my clients started our Zoom call one afternoon!

"Hard pants?"

"You know, jeans? With a zipper and a belt!"

The pandemic has changed everything, including our wardrobe and its language. Consider "mullet dressing." Business on top. Party on the bottom. Yoga pants. Athletic shorts. Sweats. Anything goes from the waist down. But from the waist up, enter the Zoom Shirt. It was "the breakout garment of the quarantine season," says Joel Stein, who made up the name for his article in *The New York Times*. He describes the Zoom Shirt as people's go-to top, "typically kept on the back of the computer chair or a hanger nearby, that they pop on in the moments before their webcam lights up. Like the pre-knotted tie President Lyndon B. Johnson kept ready to put around his neck, a Zoom Shirt instantly spiffs you up for a last-minute work meeting."[11] Or any meeting, planned or unplanned. Zoom Shirts have their equivalents: Zoom sweaters, scarfs, ties, blouses, and T-shirts worn under jackets.

While most of us have scaled back our work attire to the bare minimum since the pandemic and Zoom collided, there is a reason to consider situations where it is important to dress the part—meaning the whole suit or outfit, including shoes and accessories. That's because your clothing impacts you as much as it does others. Studies on enclothed cognition show that the clothes you wear and what they represent to you symbolically change your performance.[12]

Our wardrobe also affects how people perceive us. In a 2012 study out of the University of Kansas, participants looked at photos of shoes that other people said they wore most often and accurately judged their age, gender, income, and other attributes![13]

Dapper Dan Meet Fraser Martens

In January 2021, Fraser Martens was featured for his formal menswear in the Style and Fashion section of the *Wall Street Journal*. Fraser was an economic analyst in Moscow, Idaho, who'd been working from home for almost a year. He said he missed the structure of his commute, regular office interactions, and his cool business clothes. So, he wore chambray shirts, Brooks Brother ties, and tailored blazers to pretend things were "normal in a very abnormal year."[14]

But one abnormal year rolled into another, and Fraser's life continued to change. When I called him, he told me that he got a promotion, moved to Boise, Idaho, and he and his wife had a baby boy. His clothes changed, too. His new job is less customer-facing. "I have lots of communication on Zoom with my teammates," he said, "and they're not coat and tie people. If I wore my early pandemic clothes, it would be off-putting, and I want to have a good connection with my co-workers."

In menswear lingo, Fraser now sports "elevated workwear": corduroy pants, plaid or plain Oxford shirts, and sweaters. Sometimes a jacket. More casual but still refined, Fraser thinks of his wardrobe as part of his "professional development." He says, "It puts me in the headspace that I deserve the job I have."

If weeding out your pre-pandemic closet is like an archaeological dig, you're in good company. In November 2021, three-quarters of respondents in a survey of over 4,200 U.S. adults reported that their closets contain many items they will never wear again![15] Bags of clothes are headed to the Goodwill.

After two + years of athleisure wear, other people want to get back to glamour. In the Off Duty section of the *WSJ*, Tayna Golesic "fantasized about setting track pants on fire!"[16] Ms. Golesic is the former President of the Americas for the shoe empire, Jimmy Choo. She said, "I think people are over being boring." They're ready to ditch their Zoom shirts and get decked out. In the same article, Mercedes Posey, a clinical operations manager from Dallas, Texas, exclaimed, "Feeling like you have a reason to look great is empowering."[17]

RTO Attire

Thinking about our wardrobes can be exhausting. Now with hybrid work options, many employees see the need to bounce from WFH clothes to in-office attire.

Some people want to dress joyfully, with more color and flair, and still feel professional.

That's me. I have a power dress. It's black with occasional white, yellow, and blue flowers on the soft fabric with three-quarter length sleeves. That dress looks great on me. I love how I feel in it. Sometimes, when I'm meeting a first-time client, in person or online, or presenting to a more formal group on Zoom, I'll put that dress on and instantly feel more confident.

Are suits too stuffy for men in the workplace now? Yes and no, according to Mark Cho, who describes the new business casual in Jamie Walters' *WSJ* article.[18] Mr. Cho is the co-founder of The Armoury, a men's tailor with stores in New York and Hong Kong. Walters writes that Mr. Cho's "C-suite clients are still buying new suits for board meetings" and when needed, Walters suggests "dressing it down by pairing it with a T-shirt and smart sneakers instead of a button-down and shiny shoes."

As for what Fraser Martens is doing with his more formal business attire? He told me, "It's still waiting in my closet. Just in case."

Here's the take-away: If you feel more experienced wearing glasses, or more confident in your favorite sport coat or blazer, or more prepared when your hair looks good, beard trimmed, or makeup just right, it sends a signal to your brain to help you show up that way—more experienced, prepared, professional, and confident!

If you are interviewing, being considered for a promotion, or presenting new ideas to senior management or the Board of Directors, dress the part—even if you are on the phone. No one will see the difference, but you will feel the difference and increase your chances of presenting your best self and winning the day.

Personal Note: The Guy with the Tie

My husband, Henry, teaches Marketing, Accounting, and Personal Finance at a large, urban, public high school. With an MBA and 30+ years in business, he's used to corporate attire. Now, every day, in person or virtually, Henry teaches with a tie on. Once, a student asked him, "Hey, Mr. Hooper, why do you wear a tie?" Henry smiled, "Because I respect you that much." The student gave him a wide grin.

Color and patterns on video screens

Yes

- Neutrals, soft blues, browns. Teal, cobalt, purple, and coral pop on screen.
- Solids
- Small patterns

Avoid

- All white, all black, or bright red. They confuse the camera exposure. If it's correct on your face, your too-white top will "glow," and your skin will look darker; your too-dark top will look shapeless or "crushed." Bright reds can "bleed" on camera, giving off a hazy halo.
- Large patterns. They are distracting.
- Small, tight patterns. Even the subtlest plaid pattern or very narrow stripes can "buzz" on camera.

Modification

- White, black, or red with a vest, jacket, or scarf for balance.

No matter where you are, inside the office, WFH, or WFA, honor your company's culture. If you are customer-facing, match the culture of your client or even kick it up a notch.

Remember: It is easier to go from professional to casual than from casual to professional. Once people see you a certain way, it's hard for them to see you differently the next time. So, err on the side of professional, at least for the first "Hello."

CHAPTER 4

Presence + Posture + Power

Today, body language is more important than ever. Our movements and mannerisms let others know whether we are approachable and open to a conversation or not. But like the Nasty Resting Face, our culture doesn't promote good posture. We hunch over our cell phones and lean over laptops.

We slouch. And many people are worried about it.

Pre-pandemic, I worked on the Facebook campus, now Meta, headquartered in Menlo Park, California. It's a huge complex with twenty buildings, the largest of which has a nine-acre rooftop park with a two-and-a-half-mile jogging trail. At that time, with 10,000 employees on campus, there were topflight restaurants, a bike repair shop, a doctor's office, laundry services, and a barbershop. You name it, it was there. And of course, there was the Facebook Store with the "thumbs up" logo everywhere—on mouse pads, water bottles, and The Posture Coach. The Posture Coach? Who buys that device? Apparently, plenty of people. At that time, the cashier told me, "It's one of the most popular items in our store. You wear it on your shirt, blouse, or sweater next to your collarbone, and every time you slouch, you get a buzz to remind you to straighten up. It counts your steps, too."

Video meetings don't promote good posture, either. That's a problem for most of us because it's our primary platform to do business and connect with each other. Or, at least, try to connect. On a video call, when you hunch over your keyboard or sit with your chin propped in your hand, you can be perceived as lazy or disinterested, even if you're the most productive person on the team. You may have a casual company culture, but there's a difference between casual and sloppy.

Instant posture fix: No matter your height, stand up tall. Pull your shoulders down and away from your ears. You'll stand up straighter, and feel better, too. You can also practice this posture fix while sitting. And since they say, "sitting is the new smoking," move your body every hour and check your posture while you're at it.[1]

Health is another reason to practice good posture. Spine specialists warn us of "text neck." From texting nonstop to typing on keyboards to reading books or doing anything that strains our neck, our whole body suffers.[2]

Here's why. Your head weighs about 10 pounds. Your spine handles that pressure easily. A quick glance at your phone, the pressure rises to 27 pounds. If you're engrossed in texting, tweeting, scrolling, or answering emails, the pressure grows to 45-60 pounds. That's the average weight of an eight-year-old American child![3]

Try these techniques:

- **Stretch your neck and reset your brain**

    A few times a day, tilt your head from left to right. Slowly turn your head one way, then the other. Roll your shoulders and neck. Your muscles will thank you.

    Bring your phone to eye level instead of dropping your chin to look at your screen. It sounds simple, and it is, with practice.

- **Put it down**

    Is your smart phone the first object you look at in the morning and the last object you check before going to sleep? Join the universe. Our phones can seem like another appendage.

    Place your phone facedown, and you won't be as tempted to see what's popping up. This discipline offers rewards. Notice how much better conversations become when you're not distracted.

Buy an alarm clock. You can check the time and not be tempted to "just check my texts, emails, and Instagram."

- **Power Pose**

Good posture is "the unsung hero of confidence." It's a benefit if you're introverted, shy, reserved, or simply quiet. That's because proper posture can be your "power tool" that speaks confidence for you. It also makes you look inches taller and pounds lighter. It strengthens muscles and improves breathing. And, it sends a signal that what you say is worth hearing. If you're participating but not leading a meeting, good posture conveys that you're interested, engaged, and are fully listening.

Not convinced? Try the "Power Pose." The Power Pose was coined by social psychologist Amy Cuddy. With over 46 million views, her TED Talk is one of the world's most-watched, ever. It's called *Your Body Language May Shape Who You Are*.[4] Dr. Cuddy's research showed that people who stood for two minutes with their hands on their hips—like a superhero—or their arms raised like they'd just won a race, were rated by unknowing interviewers as more confident, intelligent, and skilled. It was as if their body was signaling to the interviewer that they had a high degree of confidence in their own abilities.[5]

Some dispute Dr. Cuddy's research as not robust or unduplicatable in further studies, but it works for me. Like a superstitious baseball player who taps his cleats before taking a swing, I Power Pose before every presentation or important call, and it makes me feel like I'm ready.

Another study at the University of British Columbia and San Francisco State University found that even blind runners throw their arms up into the air when they cross the finish line.[6] Conversely, when we feel defeated or nervous, we close ourselves off. Dr. Cuddy calls this posture a "powerlessness pose."[7]

Think about how we unconsciously assume a defensive posture when we perceive something as stressful:

- meeting someone new
- preparing for an interview, a pitch, or a presentation
- prepping for a difficult conversation in person or virtually

We often default to our phones and hunch over them when we're anxious or uncomfortable. This posture can zap our confidence and lower our professional presence before the call or conversation even begins.

How much space we take up indicates to ourselves and others how confident we feel and how competent others perceive us to be. When we feel good, we puff out our chest. We take up space. Therefore, before a crucial meeting or important event, check your posture and strike a Power Pose. It's your body's way of telling your mind, "I've got this."

The Power of Your Authentic Voice

We've highlighted the power of first impressions, including body language, clothing, grooming, facial expressions, posture, and the words you choose. But what about your voice? What if every time you spoke, you could rely on your voice to elevate your professional presence? Whether you're having an everyday conversation, a difficult discussion, or projecting in a presentation, are you confident that your authentic voice will show up and represent you well? Voice Coach Linda Brice asks, "Do you feel confident, powerful, weak, unsure? Your voice will reflect that."

Linda is a world-renowned voice coach and founder of Transformational Voice. She says, "Regardless of your profession, your speaking voice is a critical component of your self-identity. Your voice is right at the forefront of your demeanor—of how you are perceived. And your vocal demeanor is one of the most powerful tools you have to influence others."[8]

Here are three voice patterns that are unconscious and contagious and could be holding you back.

- Upspeak

- Vocal Fry

- False Deferential Voice, a.k.a. "baby voice"

Spoiler alert: You can learn skills that allow your voice to emerge naturally. With practice, these skills can transform your voice and not only make you feel more confident, but they'll also give other people more confidence in you.

Upspeak or uptalk is the habit of making declarative sentences sound like questions. For example, you put an inflection? like a question mark? any time you're speaking? even if it's in the middle of a sentence? Linguists say this causes a fully competent person to be viewed as hesitant, immature, and unconfident. It's as if they need to ask through their voice, not their words, "Is what I'm saying ok?" "Is it acceptable to you?" "I'm not rocking the boat too much, am I?" Linda says, "With upspeak, the listener sees the speaker as having no personal power."

In countries such as Australia, New Zealand, and with some people in the U.K., upspeak may sound more natural, even lyrical. But in the U.S., upspeak can send a message that you're unsure of your ideas, opinions, or the content of your presentation.

Vocal fry is another vocal epidemic. It happens when someone drops their voice into the lowest pitches that their voice can produce. It's like playing the note D on the piano, two octaves below middle C—nonstop. As a result, the speaker's vocal folds rub together and swell, and their voice fatigues fast. The lowest tones of this lowest register make the voice sound scratchy, creaky, and depressed. The Kardashians made vocal fry part of popular culture with those gravelly, raspy conversations on their reality TV shows.

Linda Brice says, "Vocal fry is an 'equal opportunity epidemic' for men and women. It's about wanting to fit into the culture. And, universally, anyone with vocal fry sounds weaker because their voice lacks energy, and inflection—the natural up and down of the voice, which is the key to influencing others."

One of my executive clients with vocal fry started working with a voice coach after his customers complained that it was hard to hear him on the phone, voicemails, and webinars. Plus, he got laryngitis regularly, which compounded the problem.

False deferential voice is the third vocal habit. It's the technical term for "baby voice." This is when grown women speak like little girls. While it can be innate for some, Linda sees it for many as an unconscious signaling that women use to convey that they are not a threat to people in power. She explains, "A woman might have a Wharton MBA, but it's too scary for her to own her power because she doesn't believe in it. So, she feels she needs to attach her coattails to someone else, and she talks like a child."

Where is your authentic voice? Is it underneath any of these vocal habits? Is it reacting to your need for approval? Your quest to fit in? Or fear? If your voice is not serving you, then Linda says, "Make a commitment to change. Not to 'fix' your voice but to transform it. It begins with self-awareness and the courage to make those changes."

Start by recording yourself. I know, it's a tough request and it's truth telling. Most people DO NOT like the sound of their own voice, even professionals! We tend to criticize our voices like we criticize our bodies, "I'm too short, too tall, too fat." That's why it's important to get neutral feedback from someone whose opinion you respect, like a trusted colleague or mentor, or a voice coach. Linda Brice says, "Often, people don't like their transformed voice until they experience the results of using it. They notice that they're holding people's attention now, they're not getting interrupted like before and they're being seen as a leader." That builds confidence.

Here are other strategies to develop your authentic voice:

- Slow down your speech. Pace has power.

- Practice the Power of Pause. This lets the listener process what you've said or prepare to hear your interesting idea or comment.

- Be definitive by using periods when you speak. Save vocal question marks with your voice for when you are truly asking a question.

- Practice recording a new voicemail greeting. Keep re-recording until it projects the vocal image you want.

- Finally, ask yourself, "Am I breathing?" Linda believes, "Breathing protects you. You can be terrified and still fuel your authentic voice by consciously breathing. Three deep breaths can get you into a meditative state to calm your nerves and strengthen your voice."

When you practice these techniques, your confidence goes up. It's not luck. It's not a whim. It's not even that you're having a good day. Like all the techniques in *The NOW Hello*, you can succeed because of concrete skills that you have learned, practiced, and put into your muscle memory.

The world needs your presence, your posture, and the power of your authentic voice.

CHAPTER 5

Camera Confidence + Connection

"The game has changed." So says professional speaker, business coach, and author Mark LeBlanc, CSP. "We have to assume that many sales conversations, presentations, meetings, negotiations and even social gatherings will be on Zoom or its equivalent for the rest of our lives."

Think about that observation. How will we adjust to Mark's prediction? How will we have effective communications through video meetings? Mark told me, "There will be more face-to-face meetings and presentations for many business professionals, though it is likely that 50% or as much as 90% of your work will be on video conferencing. Your ability to present yourself online will make or break your brand and could be how you set yourself apart from your competition."

Now is the time to practice the golden rule of The Confidence Project: "Treat everyone as if they are the most important person in the room." Because they are. And since "the room" for many professionals is now a virtual one, here are some proven ways to elevate how you present yourself on video calls with confidence.

1. Be Prompt. *"Five minutes early is on time. On time is late. Late is unacceptable."*

Being prompt seems elementary, but it's essential. It shows respect for the team, the prospect, or the client. It boosts your credibility and shows that you're organized and efficient. And, now more than ever, with the world's colliding crises—including health, the economy, racial reckoning, education, conflict, and our climate—being on time demonstrates that you are highly thoughtful of others.

Just because many people still aren't commuting to work every day doesn't guarantee our being on time for meetings. You can be twenty steps away from your home office and still be late for virtual meetings. Leave space between video calls to account for unexpected tech issues, children or pet problems, or even for a bio break. Plus, ten minutes to prepare for a meeting or decompress afterwards will keep you calmer. Show up on time and be ready.

2. Be Present.

It's easy to be distracted with a laptop on your desk, a separate monitor, notifications pinging, and your cell phone nearby, face up. We all know the "eye angle" when someone pretends as if they're paying attention, but really, they're checking emails, answering texts, or ordering take-out from Chipotle. We're all guilty at some point or another. The best way to be present is to stay focused on one conversation at a time and not be tempted to multitask.

Multitasking is overrated. When you juggle texts, emails, music, and Zoom calls, your productivity drops. According to a study out of the University of London, your IQ drops too! By an average of fifteen points. How does that translate? Those multitaskers "experienced IQ score declines that were similar to what they'd expect if they had smoked marijuana or stayed up all night."[1]

Further, "IQ drops of 15 points for multitasking men lowered their scores to the average range of an eight-year-old child."[2] Be present, focus on one task at a time, and you'll be smarter, too!

Zoom rewards you.

In Zoom, if you want to be noticed by the leader, client, or other attendees, turn your camera on.

The reward: Your face shows up on the first page.

If it's a large crowd, you'll appear on the first few pages. For those showing their name or headshot only, the Zoom algorithm moves them to the last pages.

The result: Those folks may not be noticed or remembered for being on the call.

---

3. Keep Your Camera On.

There's neuroscience to support this finding. When your camera is turned on and you see someone's face, you get a dose of dopamine, one of the happy hormones, like serotonin and oxytocin. And that dose provides invisible energy.

Keeping your camera on, however, can be controversial.

During the first summer of the pandemic, I was participating on the local board of a national organization. We were planning an upcoming meeting with a guest presenter from NYC. Virtual, of course. As we wrapped up the session, I suggested, "You know, it's hard enough to present in person, but at least in person you feel energy from people in the room. On WebEx or Teams, with people in muted boxes, it takes a lot more energy to present. Plus, you don't get much feedback from the audience. So, I request, as a courtesy to our presenter, that all board members keep our cameras on."

Whoa. Sparks started flying!

"Do you see my background? It's my refrigerator. My kitchen is my office."

"Who noticed my 15-year-old son walk behind me?"

"We have terrible Wi-Fi at our house, so I have to keep my camera off to have decent audio."

I felt awful, as if I had offended everybody. But to my surprise, at the next meeting, every board member had their camera on. From my perspective, that showed our gratitude and esteem for the speaker and everyone else at the meeting.

Camera: On. Off. On.

To give people a break from constantly being on camera, one of my clients worked out an arrangement with his team and regular clients for long meetings. At the start, they turn on their cameras to greet each other. They turn them off to share documents full screen. Back on if there's a substantive issue to discuss. Off to continue sharing. Finally, cameras back on at the end to say thank you and goodbye.

One of my clients, who is an SVP at a national bank, felt she was losing connection with her team because they kept their cameras off during meetings. It was hard enough to work during a pandemic, so for months, she never said anything. Finally, she admitted, "I miss seeing your faces! I'd love it if you'd turn your cameras on." Presto! Faces appeared! Her simple request made all the difference, especially since her team is still working remotely.

4. Lift Your Laptop.

Without a standing desk or an adjustable stand to raise your laptop, most devices sit below your chin.

Note: There may be three supermodels in the world who look striking when photographed from below, but for the rest of us, it's not a good look! The people on the call are looking up into our nostrils! Or at our ceiling fan. (My brother Tom says, "I never knew there were so many ceiling fans!")

You can fix that. Lift your laptop until the camera is at eye level or slightly above.

Perhaps the biggest incentive to raise your device is to avoid "chin cam." That's the dreaded double chin that is exposed when we look down at our screen! Dr. Alan Matarasso is a plastic surgeon in NYC. He reported that when the COVID-19 quarantine began, his office "received many more queries about double chin reductions, including tucks and liposuction."[3]

It turns out that in The World of Work now, with more video conferencing than ever, the "under-the-chin girth" is glaringly obvious when people lean over their laptops. Poorly positioned webcams can add ten pounds under your jawline. Some people are resorting to a low-tech solution: pulling back their skin with clear Scotch tape! I suggest a more professional fix. Start with good posture and adjust your camera angle instead!

Sit on a steady chair. Swivel chairs are comfortable, but we tend to . . . swivel. And that's distracting.

5. Look into the Lens.
Spot the dot on your computer. If you want to make everyone feel as if they are the most important person in the room, look into the lens with the green, red, or white dot next to the camera.

Looking into the lens is a skill that takes practice to master, and it is worth it.

I learned the value of this technique in my early TV news days at WBAL in Baltimore, Maryland. I worked with a talented videographer named Pete Greer. One day, when we were shooting a stand-up, I said to Pete, "It feels weird to look into the camera and not see anything. It's like a dark hole."

Pete said, "Here's the trick. Picture someone you love on the other side of the camera."

I thought, "OK, I love my mom. I'll talk to her!" So, from then on, for stand-ups and live shots, I looked into the camera, pictured my mother on the other side and told her the news story.

Try it. When you're on a webinar, imagine that you're speaking to someone you trust, admire, or care about. It will help people on the call to connect with you.

Here's another reason to look into the lens.

Early in the pandemic, I was on a Zoom call with an experienced HR director at an international events company. When he was hired in January 2020, the company was booming. They had 1000+ employees in over 40 locations worldwide. Business was booked through the end of 2022. Then came COVID. Overnight their business was decimated. And so began this HR executive's nightmare: endless, painful video calls to lay off colleagues who he'd never met.

As he described the heartbreaking conversations, I noticed that he looked down at me on his screen.

"Those calls must be horrible for you," I said.

"They are. I've been in HR for twenty years, and I've never had to let people go on such a large scale."

"Would you mind if I offered some spot coaching to help with those calls?"

"Sure. Please. I'll take any support you can give me."

"Look into your lens. It's as close as you can get to making someone feel as if you are looking directly at them to deliver the bad news."

He paused to consider my advice. Then he said, "I know I should do that, but I depend on seeing people's body language and facial expressions, and I can't read their reactions when I'm looking into the camera."

"I hear you. You can glance down at your screen to see their faces and read those nonverbals. You can also briefly look at the screen while they're speaking to see their body language cues. Then, look back up at the camera. With practice, you can look into the lens and develop a kind of peripheral vision below your eyes to see their faces. Do the best you can to keep that connection. It's powerful, and they'll feel it."

Pro Tip

For a visual cue, take a Post-it Note, draw an arrow, and write, "Look here!" Or put a small photo of your favorite animal who looks at you lovingly and never talks back! Stick it next to the "dot" to remind yourself that there's a real person on the other side of that camera who's getting a dollop of dopamine when they see you "looking" through the lens right into their eyes.

---

6. Your Mic is Always Open.

For nearly half a century, whenever someone was eager to break into broadcasting in Baltimore, Maryland, they'd try to find their way to my father, Vince Bagli. He was known as the "Dean of Sports." Here's the most important piece of advice Dad ever gave: "Remember, your mic is always open."

Here's an example straight out of my current on-camera life.

Before presentations, I log on 15 minutes early to greet the client, set up my slide deck, and do a tech check. My camera is off, and I am on mute. Before one presentation, I heard a participant spewing expletives about not being able to find his virtual background.

"Where is my *bleeping* background? *Expletive. Expletive. Bleep.* I had it ready last night, and now I can't find the *bleeping* thing."

He didn't realize his mic was open. Several of his colleagues had logged on and heard his rant. I thought, "I gotta save this guy from himself." So I unmuted my mic, turned on my camera, and helped him find his background.

Once he realized his mic was open during his tirade, he was mortified and told me later, "I guess I didn't remember your dad's sage advice. 'Your mic is always open.'"

Another way to protect yourself from "open mic" slip-ups is to align your words with your actions in any public or professional setting. As Warren Buffett has said, "It takes twenty years to build a reputation and five minutes to ruin it. If you think about that, you'll do things differently."

Drag It
When you reference content during a video meeting, drag the information over to the same screen as your camera. Otherwise, with the information on a separate monitor, you'll be looking away from the camera and anyone on the call.

---

7. Nix the Noise.
Our world is noisy enough. We don't need to hear another ping! When a notification or news alert goes off on your phone or laptop, whether in person or in a virtual meeting,

it's the equivalent of interrupting the speaker. It's rude. Worse yet, if you're the speaker who's presenting, those noises are distracting and can break everybody's concentration. Turn off your notifications. Honor the audience of 1 or 100.

Allow for Accommodations
When I was coaching an IT executive to better connect with people by looking into the lens, he shared his challenge. "I'm dyslexic and it's easier for me to look at the screen to read people's lips." His technique was a literal eye-opener for me.

Here's where flexibility meets confidence. Looking into the lens is a guideline. If it doesn't work for you, modify it. That's the foundation of resilient confidence. You can always be confident knowing you are doing your best.

---

8. Background.
If you don't have a neutral wall or your workspace is small or cluttered, consider using the Zoom blur with your current background. You could also buy a collapsible, portable green screen to display any number of cool photo options. A green screen uses chromakey technology to superimpose your image onto a virtual background of your choice. If you use a virtual background without a green screen, part of your

face, hair, hands, and body can look like they are separating from each other. It's distracting and amateurish. You can buy a green screen online and instantly have a background with a professional look.

Note: Microsoft Teams doesn't require a green screen. It has a built-in tool for filtering out the background. Its shortcoming is that the images are static.

If you have the space, skip the green screen, and consider buying a large roll of vinyl, seamless wallpaper. You'll need a wall mount or stand, or you can attach it to your ceiling. There are hundreds of background options from playful to professional. If the price is right, buy more than one and change it up, depending on the situation.

If it's in your budget, consider buying an external camera. The camera embedded in your computer is tiny and cannot provide good quality video and audio. Since, as Mark LeBlanc says, we'll be "Zooming" forever, it's important that you look good and sound clear. With a quality external camera, you can feel confident that your professional presence is improved to the 2.0 virtual version.

9. Lighting.

If you know a photographer or lighting pro, hire them. And even if you don't know a pro, research, check customer reviews, and hire an expert. It's worth the investment to create the best lighting for your skin color, balding head, background, or room with or without windows. If you wear glasses, the pros have tricks to help avoid seeing the glare in your lenses. And if you're bald, they have techniques to help keep the glare off your head.

If it's absolutely not in your budget to hire a photographer, you'll look best if your light source is in front of you or balanced on either side of your laptop. Or both. Experiment. The pros say that artificial light is best because it's consistent. If you need to boost the brightness in your home office, a ring light is a popular, inexpensive solution. However, how many times have you seen a ring light reflected in the glasses of a presenter? Here's a helpful trick. Wrap the ring light with parchment paper. You can find it in the baking aisle at the grocery store. This trick softens the brightness. It also can keep the ring light from reflecting in your glasses.

There are plenty of YouTube videos for a D.I.Y. approach to setting up your workspace. Many videos offer inexpensive ways to upgrade your office. Be creative to find the best result. Ultimately, with a more professional setting, you'll feel more confident.

A reason to look away, briefly.
If you're leading the call, tell people at the start, "I'll be referencing material on another monitor. So if I look away, it's because I'm looking at the information on the other screen. I'm still listening to you."

10. Eating and Drinking.

I advise no eating. Eat before or after your calls. Drinking coffee, water, or other non-alcoholic beverages during a business call is fine. Here's a page from the professional speakers' handbook. In our industry, we're taught, "Don't let anything stand between you and the audience. No podium. No desk. No table."

But what about a coffee mug? When you take a sip, the mug can cover your whole face. That gesture separates you from others on the call. Instead, keep your eyes on the camera and turn your head slightly to the side. Or look away briefly so you can sip your drink and your cup isn't blocking your face. You can use a straw, too. It's subtle and savvy.

People may not be able to identify why they're comfortable with you on a video call. It doesn't matter. It's another non-verbal cue that shows you're present, you value the person on the call, and they can trust you.

Everything starts at 'the 5.'

Rich Barton learned this tip from Matt Mullenweg. Rich is the Founder of Zillow, the most-visited real estate website in the U.S.; Matt Mullenweg is the CEO of Automattic, the all-remote parent company of WordPress.

Here's how "The 5" works: Every meeting BEGINS five minutes after the hour (2:05 p.m.) or half-hour (2:35 p.m.), and every meeting ENDS on the half-hour (2:30 p.m.) or hour (3 p.m.) The same holds true for 55-minute meetings. This technique helps reduce burnout. It gives people a few moments to pet their dog, do some burpees, or use the restroom before the next meeting starts.[4]

Lower Anxiety and Manage Energy

For some people, preparing for and being on video calls can make them feel anxious. Thanks to my on-camera experience, advice from other professional speakers, and a Harvard study, I mix and match a variety of techniques to prepare for high-stakes meetings and presentations. Choose your favorites.

- **Use the Power Pose.** I stand for two minutes with my hands on my hips.[5]

- **Make a mental movie.** During the Power Pose, I picture how well the call or presentation will go. And how empowered people will feel when they learn and practice these confidence boosting techniques.

- **Take deep belly breaths.** Keith Golden is a Movement and Breathing Coach in Baltimore, Maryland. He told me, "To calm your nervous system and lower your blood pressure, take a deep breath in through your nose, expanding from your belly up through your chest, for a count of four seconds. Then, slowly breathe out for four seconds through your mouth. To get more relaxed, gradually lengthen each exhale until it's twice as long as the inhale; four beats in; eight beats out. This technique is helpful first-thing in the morning or before a big presentation or meeting." Make it a regular part of your day. We need to breathe anyway. We might as well use our breath to help us "keep calm and carry on!"

- **Rub your Achilles tendons.** A physical reaction is best handled with a physical action according to The Brain Gym® Program.[6] Physical reactions like a quivering voice, flushed cheeks, or perspiration can dissipate when you relax your Achilles. Diane Allen is a professional violinist and flow state expert. She told me that this calming technique is key to her success. Diane suffered from trembling hands, a liability for anyone who performs on a high-precision instrument. No more. Now, she massages her Achilles ahead of a performance and performs with confidence.

- Read affirmations and motivating quotes aloud. Before a presentation, I read a collection of inspiring words from my "Get Psyched" folder. And I add new ones regularly.

- Say out loud, "I'm excited" vs. "I'm anxious." This technique of reframing performance anxiety as excitement was researched by Alison Wood Brooks, a professor at Harvard Business School. She wanted to see how self-talk could influence a person's singing accuracy when performing karaoke. Participants were asked to sing the first verse of Journey's "Don't Stop Believin'," the 21st most downloaded song in iTunes history! It turns out that the participants who said out loud "I'm excited" reported feeling significantly more excited before singing. Plus, their lyric accuracy was over 80 percent![7]

Flex your observer muscle.
If you're not the presenter and you have data to share, put a link in the chat for everyone to see. Or request screen sharing to present your content with the meeting participants.

Finally, Zoom Fatigue

One time, on what felt like the 100th Zoom call of the week, the host announced, "I am so sick of seeing myself!" Then someone else jumped in, "Same here. My goal these days is to go to a meeting where I don't have to look at my own face!" Finally, someone sighed, "I'm exhausted every day." Welcome to Zoom Fatigue.[8]

No offense to Zoom. It's just that Zoom has become the generic name for video calls like Kleenex to tissue and Saran Wrap to plastic wrap. Zoom, WebEx, Skype, FaceTime, WhatsApp, Google Meet, Microsoft Teams, whatever platform you use, being "always on" is exhausting and physically draining. Even Eric Yuan, the CEO of Zoom, admits to Zoom Fatigue but refers to it as Meeting Fatigue! Either way, he says he doesn't schedule back-to-back meetings anymore.[9]

"Virtual interactions can be extremely hard on the brain," says Dr. Andrew Franklin, assistant professor of cyberpsychology at Norfolk State University in Virginia in a *National Geographic* article. According to Dr. Franklin, humans communicate even when we're quiet.[10] When you're face-to-face with someone, you focus on the words and also dozens of nonverbal cues. Are they looking at you or turned away? Is their head slightly cocked? Are they frowning? Smiling? This is how we connect with each other.

But on video calls, we miss a lot of those cues because screens are small and one-dimensional with lots of heads squeezed into a grid. It's tough to detect how people are responding when someone is framed from the shoulders up and we can't see their hands or read other body language. Dr. Franklin says, "The brain becomes overwhelmed searching for non-verbal cues that it can't find."[11] The Gallery View, showing everyone on screen "challenges the brain's 'central vision,' forcing it to decode so many people at once, that no one comes through meaningfully, not even the speaker," continues Dr. Franklin.[12]

Add unstable internet connections, half-second delays, and distractions like your cat with its l-o-n-g tail walking behind you in the frame and it's no wonder we're in overdrive trying to connect and stay productive.

Here are three strategies to help manage Zoom Fatigue.

1. **Less is more!** Shorten your video calls. With a clear and tight agenda, you can get much accomplished in 15-20 minutes.

2. **Use the good ol' telephone** . . . the most underused tech tool of the 21st century. Consider follow-ups or even holding meetings by phone. I'm a note-taker, so when I'm on a video call, I always tell people, "I'm taking notes, so if I look away, don't worry, I'm still paying attention to you." On the phone, nobody sees me writing. I don't have to be "on." I can listen, take notes, and respond. Or, if I don't need to take notes, I can walk and talk and get in my 10,000 steps!

3. Create intentional transitions. Pre-COVID, we'd go from building to building or down the hall or travel from one part of town to another for conferences, networking events, or other meetings. Those natural transitions allowed us to decompress or prepare for the next face-to-face. Now, for anyone still working remotely with back-to-back video calls, you may feel the need to say, "Do you mind if I step away to take a bite of lunch before we get started?" or "Sorry. I need a few minutes to use the restroom!"

Try this: Take 10-15 minutes to transition from one video call to the next. Step outside. Make a cup of tea. Do a set of squats. Or sing along to your favorite playlist.

Power nap.
If Margaret Thatcher, Winston Churchill, John F. Kennedy, Thomas Edison, Salvador Dali, Leonardo da Vinci, Albert Einstein, and Eleanor Roosevelt could take power naps and still be highly successful, so can you. A micro nap can help revive your mind and body.

Setting boundaries around your schedule shows confidence. Encourage your colleagues to do the same. Don't take a rare break. Take a real break.

Take a blink break for 20:20:20.
Besides being mentally taxing, our eyes can get dry and irritated from endless screen time.

Dr. Mila Ioussifova is an Optometrist & Dry Eye Specialist.[13] She told me that we should be blinking about fifteen times every minute because blinking lubricates our eyes. When we stare at our screens all day and binge on Netflix at night, Dr. Mila says, we only blink 4-5 times a minute! The result: our hard-working eyes can get that aching, burning, scratchy feeling.

Take a Blink Break.

Dr. Mila says, "Every 20 minutes look at something 20 feet away and blink 20 times. Close your eyes, slightly squeeze, then open. Close. Squeeze. Open. Repeat until your eyes feel more relaxed."

While you're taking a Blink Break, sip some green tea. Its antioxidants can help your eyes produce tears for better lubrication!

As a leader, you can model this technique to encourage your team to take care of themselves. When you offer something practical like a Blink Break, it communicates to your team that you care about them, their health, and their well-being. It's a small, out-of-the-box Model & Teach approach to leadership.

Take care of yourself. Your productivity will increase. And, your brain and your colleagues will thank you.

CHAPTER 6

Words to LOSE + Words to USE

We've covered plenty of material on how to show up and look your best online or in person. But once you've arrived at your destination—digitally or face-to-face—how can you best express yourself? In this chapter, we'll discuss how to use language in your interactions that will elevate your professional presence. We'll cover **Words to LOSE** that are overused, ineffective, and sound hesitant or weak. And, we'll offer ways to replace them with **Words to USE** that are strong and have influence and impact. These **Words to USE** will impact your ability to be seen and heard. In short, **Words to USE** are worthy of you.[1]

What Influences Our Language and Word Choice?

1. Habit. If we're comfortable with how we speak and we don't get feedback, we keep talking that way. It's easy. It's safe.

2. Culture. What we hear, we say—unconsciously, of course. We want to fit in with the culture, so we tend to imitate what we hear. We want to belong.

3. Fear. Voice expert Linda Brice shared this with me: "Our biggest fear is that we will be shamed, humiliated, or banished from the group when we speak up. So, we freeze and can't access our thoughts. And we literally stop breathing. While we stand there, madly trying to gather our ideas, we use various words to mask our anxiety."[2]

Habit, Culture, and Fear keep people locked into using Words to LOSE that can chip away at your Confidence and dilute your message. Words such as

Fillers

- Uh
- Umm
- Like
- You know
- Whatever
- And again
- Go ahead and
- Stuff
- Thing
- Wow
- OK
- So

You may recognize the first several Fillers as the usual suspects. But what about the expression *go ahead and* . . . This is a trendy throwaway line, and it doesn't add value to what you're saying.

Lose: Go ahead and start the project.
Use: You can start the project anytime.

Lose: Go ahead and text me when you're ready.
Use: Please text me when you're ready.

Lose: Let me go ahead and make the appointment.
Use: I'll make the appointment.

Stuff

Stuff is what could be in your hall closet, kitchen junk drawer, or garbage bin. When we speak about stuff in business, it sounds sloppy and vague.

Lose: I know my stuff.
Use: I know my material, my topic, the data.

Lose: We have a lot of stuff to discuss.
Use: We have six topics to discuss.
   We have an action-packed agenda.

Thing

By *thing*, do you mean technique, discipline, habit, principle, an idea, concern, goal, problem, outcome, or takeaway?

When top executive speech coach Patricia Fripp works with her clients, here is the question she most frequently asks them, "If it were not a thing, what would it be?"[3]

One brilliant engineer said, "There are two *things* people love about . . . "

After her question, he said, "*Innovative upgrades.*"

She kept on, "There are billions of people in the world. What *people* love your innovative upgrades?"

He smiled, "*Systems administrators.*"

Can you see the difference that specific language makes? Patricia Fripp says, "Specificity builds credibility."

Lose: The thing is
Use: The goal is

Lose: Here's the thing.
Use: Here's the issue, problem, situation.

Lose: We need to focus on every little thing.
Use: We need to focus on every single detail.

Wow

Wow is a part of popular culture. Owen Wilson has made Wow! famous by using it incessantly in his movies. (Watch YouTube's compilation![4]) I suggest you save Wow! for a truly wow experience. It will have a bigger impact.

So

So is one of those Fillers that I'm working to LOSE. It's a wind-up word, as if you are going to start from the very beginning. "So, here's what happened . . . So, it seemed like a good idea . . . So, let's start with . . . So, the next time . . . So, if you are interested . . . So, I suggest . . . "

I never knew that "so" was one of my weak words until I was preparing to be a guest on a Portland TV show called *Afternoon Live*. After the producer and I discussed the topic, I suggested a list of questions for the host. The week before, I started practicing my answers. When I practice, I call it "a shelfie!" I put my cell phone on a bookshelf, press record, and rehearse the conversation. Here's what surprised me. In that mock, 6-minute interview, I used the word "so" 13 times! That's nearly once every 30 seconds.

I was using "so" as a way of giving myself a second to think about my answer or to tie my thoughts together. It's a habit. Like most of the Fillers, the only solution is to drop the word. Practice is key.

Power of Pause

If you catch yourself overusing Fillers or any of the following Words to LOSE, practice the Power of Pause.

Successful comedians use this technique. Right before delivering a punch line, they pause. You can too. This slight break will give you a chance to choose your words. It will also help the listener process what you've already said or prepare them for the great idea or comment that you're about to offer.

Hedges

- Just
- Kind of
- Sort of
- A little
- Almost
- Maybe
- I guess
- Actually
- Pretty
- Lucky

Linguists call these small, sneaky add-on words Hedges because it's as if the speaker is hedging to appear less aggressive, domineering, demanding, or overbearing.[5] Instead of being straightforward, they hedge and sound hesitant. These common Words to LOSE soften your delivery and can undercut your message.

One of the most overused Hedges is *just*. How often have you written or said, "I'm just checking back" (as a soft nudge) or "I just have a quick question" (to tee up a request) or "Just wondering if you've decided about . . ." (asking for an answer or permission). Or, if you fear being interrupted, "I just want to say really fast?" Here it's as if we feel we need to cram a lot of words together, so we don't get talked over.

Of course, there are times when it's perfectly normal to use just.

- "I was just thinking about you."
- "Her book has just been published."
- "That is just the right amount of cinnamon for my latte."

If you need to nudge or send a reminder, instead of saying, "Just checking in on the information," use your "I Statements" and say with a matter-of-fact tone,

Hi Jim,

The client proposal is due by end-of-day Monday. For me to finish it, I need the information from your office two-days ahead. When can I expect it, please?

Thanks,
Ellen

Just Sayin'

Early one winter morning, I was walking home from the gym, which was a few blocks from our house. I had to cross a four-lane road, but it was safe with a traffic light. The walk signal flashed, and when I got to the other side, I heard a voice calling, "Hey? Hello?" I looked across the street. A driver who was waiting for the light to turn green had rolled down his window and said, "It's really dark out here and you're wearing all black, so it's super hard to see you. You should get one of those reflector vests." I waved, "Thanks a lot. I'll do that!" Then he said, "Just sayin'." I thought, "Just sayin'?" That guy might have saved my life because now at dawn or dusk, I wear a reflector vest when I walk. He didn't need to justify what he said.

Do these other Hedges sound familiar?

- I'm *a little* concerned about the client's commitment to working with us because they keep postponing our meetings.

- I *kind of* think the proposal should be reorganized.

- I *almost* feel like we should go back to square one.

- *Maybe* we should consider more research.

- I *guess* I wonder if we are underestimating the impact of our decision.

- I'm *actually* ready to take on more responsibility. (It's as if you're surprised.)

- I'm *pretty* prepared for this meeting.

- I'm a *pretty* skilled negotiator, or *pretty* creative, *pretty* good at sales, marketing, or business development.

Read these sentences without the Hedges. They are stronger, more definitive. The Power of Pause will come in handy to help you to LOSE Hedges.

Ask a trusted friend or colleague if they'd be willing to record your conversation. Tell them you want to lose some weak words to improve your communication. Chances are, they'll be curious about their own Words to LOSE, too.

At first, you both may be overly conscious of every word you say, but after a few minutes, you'll speak as you normally do. That's when the typical Words to LOSE will come right out of your mouths! On the playback, listen for those repeated words, patterns, and phrases. And practice losing them.

Agree to be Accountability Partners to keep the learning alive.

A few years ago, I was advising a senior executive in her mid-40s who'd achieved great success in her tech company.

When we met, she said, "*You know*, I know my *stuff* and I'm *pretty good* at what I do. But lately, we've been hiring a lot of young talent, and I *just* feel like I'm not being taken seriously. *Like*—people don't see how capable I am. And it's *sort of* rattling my confidence *a little. You know what I mean?*"

Think about that statement. In five sentences that fully competent professional used eight individual or groups of Words to LOSE. She'd lost perspective on her worth and began to feel, as she said, "invisible." To counter that perception, we upgraded her vocabulary.

I asked, "Do you have a sticky note?"

"Sure."

"Good. Let's change up your language to be more strategic. Write down these phrases:"

- From my perspective . . .
- What I know (after 15 years in the tech industry or at this company) . . .
- Our data shows . . .
- I recommend (as in, I recommend we accept this proposal)

Then I said, "Put that sticky note on the upper corner of your laptop. Whenever you talk on the phone, in person, on a Zoom call, or by email, use those words."

One Thursday afternoon she called me with a lilt in her voice. "Tracy, it's crazy! In two weeks, people started listening to me differently. It's as if I have more credibility and influence."

"You always have," I said, "but now your words match your capabilities."

Words have power.

Post-it

Write three phrases or Words to USE on a Post-it. Stick it to the corner of your computer. And every time you're on the phone, on a video call, or writing an email, replace the words you would typically say with your new Words to USE. As you get more skilled at using these Words to USE, you'll begin to say them naturally when talking with people face to face.

> *"Luck is not a strategy."*
> – SETH GODIN[6]

In 2013, Lauren McGoodwin launched a website called Career Contessa.[7] It's a resource specifically for women and work; however, I feel the information is helpful for any professional.

As Lauren was telling me how they developed the website, she said, "In the beginning, we were lucky to—" She stopped mid-sentence, "No. We were smart to . . ." And she finished her thought. Lauren course-corrected right in the middle of her comment. She and her team were not lucky. Winning the lottery is lucky. Finding a primo parking spot is lucky. Their team is "smart." You are, too.

> *"I am not lucky. You know what I am? I am smart. I am talented. I take advantage of the opportunities that come my way and I work really, really hard. Don't call me lucky."*[8]
> — SHONDA RHIMES
> American TV producer, screenwriter, creator: *Grey's Anatomy, Scandal* and *Bridgerton*

Confident or Cocky

For people who worry, "How do I sound confident but not cocky," Dictionary.com makes the distinction.

Cock•y
adjective
    Arrogant; pertly self-assertive; conceited.[9]

Con·fi·dent
adjective
> Sure of oneself; having no uncertainty about one's own abilities; correctness, successfulness, etc.[10]

Several years ago, I had a great conversation with a man who'd had a fantastic career with an international athletic apparel company. When I asked him, "Tell me what your strengths are," he smiled and with a pleasant tone said, "I'm an expert at leading large global teams." Bam. Straight forward. No arrogance or conceit. No Hedges to seem humble. He was matter of fact and it was uplifting. You can express yourself the same way. Open body language + neutral tone + pleasant expression = confident not cocky.

Disclaimers

Linguists say people use Disclaimers to seem humble or modest. But they don't make you sound confident. Instead, they sound self-deprecating and can dampen your voice. Disclaimers can also be perceived as false humility.

> **Lose:** Correct me if I'm wrong.
> *Why would we ask someone to correct us before we start talking?*
> **Use:** Let me know if I heard this correctly. (Or simply start talking.)

Lose: You've been doing this longer.
That may be true, but you may bring a fresh perspective.
Use: In my experience,

Lose: Jump in if you think I'm missing something.
Don't assume they'll find something missing. Ask for comments or opinions when you are ready, either during your presentation or after you've finished talking.
Use: Feel free to share your thoughts after I present my idea.

Here's what I'm thinking. Tell me if you agree with it.

Here's what I'm thinking . . . How are we doing so far?

Feel free to add any additional details or steps.

Is there anything else we need to cover or talk about?

Have I considered everything in this transaction or process?

Now, let's open it up for comments and suggestions.

Lose: What do I know? or I could be way off-base.
You know more than you think. Trust your experience and success. You could also be spot on.
Use: Here's my perspective.

Lose: I could be over-thinking this.
Everyone's brain perceives differently. It's called being a human.
Use: Let's dig deeper.

Lose: This is just my 2 cents.
That's brainstorming.
Use: What if we try this . . .

Lose: This may sound like a crazy idea, *or* This might not be a bad idea.
More brainstorming!
Use: Let's consider . . .

Lose: Here's a stupid question. Or as I heard a serious journalist say to a guest on their program, "Apologies for asking a stupid question."
No question is stupid. No need to ask for forgiveness here.
Use: Here's my question.

Here's a starter, elementary, foundational, fundamental question.

Or, as I heard Michael Barbaro ask a guest on his podcast, *The Daily*, "Walk us through that in an Econ 101 manner . . ."[11]

Lose: You can poke holes in this, or you can throw this away . . .
Why solicit criticism?
Use: I suggest this.
Here's my suggestion.
What do you think of this plan?

Common Disclaimers from Some Younger Professionals

Lose: I have no idea what I'm talking about.
I believe you do have some idea. Say it.
Use: I have an idea and I'd like to run it by you.

Lose: This is totally just my opinion.
You don't have to justify your opinion. Trust yourself and tell us.
Use: This is my opinion.
Here's my perspective.

Lose: I don't really know, buuut . . .
Nix the negative.
Use: Here's an option for us to consider. What do you think?

Lose: You probably don't want to do this, but . . .
Assume the positive.
Use: I have a proposal. What if we . . .

Lose: Maybe it's just me, but . . .
It's likely not just you.
Use: Simply say it.

"This thought is 30 seconds old!"

If you feel you need to use a "set-up phrase," try my mother Barbara's. She says, "This thought is 30 seconds old!" Then, she launches right into it. Barbara knows her idea is not fully formed, but she's confident enough to share it anyway.

Check in with yourself. Does using these Disclaimers and other Words to LOSE come from a deeper place of insecurity or fear? Do you feel as if you're not worthy of making a statement without a set-up phrase? Is it cultural? (As one client told me, "I grew up being told, 'Don't brag. Don't promote yourself.'") Is this the language you heard your elders or authority figures say when you were young? Or are these Words to LOSE simply your habitual way of communicating or wanting to belong? If so, read on. You can change your language and the narrative in your head. You are worthy of your voice, your opinion, and your success.

Confidence is contagious.

As you begin to adopt these Words to USE and hear them come out of your mouth, you'll start to feel more confident. In turn, others will begin to have more confidence in you. It is a virtuous cycle upward!

Convincers

These Words to LOSE are ways we try to soften our delivery or a hard truth. But they end up sounding more like confessions or excuses. This way of speaking doesn't promote trust. It also doesn't demonstrate your credibility and capabilities.

> **Lose:** "*Not gonna lie.* This was a difficult project, and I didn't have enough support up or down." (Confession)
> **Use:** "*Here's how it was.* This was a difficult project, and I didn't have enough support up or down. I'd like to talk about how I can get more assistance going forward."

> **Lose:** "*Full transparency.* Saskia finished the report because on Sunday my dog and I went on a hike, and he must have stepped on something because he started limping. So, I called my Vet first thing on Monday, but they didn't have an opening until 11 a.m. . . . " (Excuse)

Use: "*Here's what happened.* I had a personal issue to attend to. Saskia finished the report, and she did a great job. Thanks, Saskia."

Lose: "*Trust me.* It's going to be easier to collaborate when we're all back in the office." (Trying to convince)
Use: As a team, we need to collaborate, and I feel we can do that more effectively in person in the office." (Simply make your statement.)

Lose: "*To be honest,* we're running behind schedule. We can't get the proposal to you for a few more days." (As if you're not always honest?)
Use: "*You can feel confident* that we will have the proposal ready for your review by EOD, Thursday."

> TBH (To be honest) joins air fryer, deplatform, and dad bod as three of the 455 newest words and definitions added to Merriam-Websters Dictionary in 2021![12]

Exaggerators and Absolutes

These are overused words that are intentionally extreme. They devalue our statements because the listener doesn't know what weight to give them.

Exaggerators are trendy, over-the-top cliches, and therefore unbelievable. You can be truthful and sincere without exaggerating.

Exaggerators:
- Amazing!
- Awesome!
- Incredible!
- Super!

Lose: That report was amazing!
Use: That report was well-organized and researched.

Lose: What an awesome off-site.
Use: The off-site was an excellent use of our time away from the office. I appreciated the training, and the non-scheduled time was great, too. I got to reconnect with a lot of people.

Lose: Your contribution to the project was incredible!
Use: Your contribution to the project was exactly what we needed to impress the client. Your PowerPoint and examples demonstrated our division's value.

Lose: Your report was super organized!
Use: I'm impressed with how well you organized that report. Will you send me your outline? I'd like to share it with the team as a template for upcoming projects.

Absolutes are often inaccurate because they leave no leeway for an alternate choice. We use these words to make a point, but they can backfire because they are not always true.

Always

Lose: "These Monday morning meetings always run over."
Use: "I notice that these Monday morning meetings frequently/often/usually run over."

Never

Lose: "We can never get the numbers right."
Use: I've noticed that we rarely/seldom/hardly ever/infrequently get the numbers right."
Use: We need to consistently get the numbers right.

Validators

People use Validators such as "Do you know what I mean?" to check in with their audience. Or to get buy-in from them. Research shows, however, that when we use these phrases, we are seen as less influential and less knowledgeable about a topic even when we are fully competent. This is especially true for women.[13]

It's important to understand the context in which your language is used. When I was leading a training at a large law firm, one of the senior partners said, "We practice Family Law. We advise clients about divorce, alimony, child support, estates, retirement benefits. It's complicated, intense, and can get emotional. So, to make sure they're getting it, I often ask my clients, 'Does that make sense?' or 'Am I being clear?'"

I understand. For instance, if you're a banker, accountant, architect, attorney, financial planner, engineer, a supply chain or IT expert, or physician, your work is complex and you need to be sure your clients, customers, or patients understand your message. But when you pause during a conversation to make sure you are connecting with others, consider substituting with these Words to Use:

>**Lose:** Does that make sense? *Or* Am I making sense?
>**Use:** Do you have any questions?

>**Lose:** Am I being clear?
>**Use:** Do I need to clarify anything?
>Let me know if I can clarify something for you.

>**Lose:** Is that OK?
>**Use:** What are your thoughts?

>**Lose:** See what I'm saying?
>**Use:** How's this landing with you?
>Does anyone want to weigh in?
>Let me know if you'd like me to repeat anything.

>**Lose:** Do you know what I mean?
>**Use:** Do you have any comments?
>Raise your hand if this resonates with you.
>What's coming up for you?
>I'd appreciate your feedback.

Hidden Negatives & Clear Positives

Have you noticed that some business discussions and even everyday conversations have become laced with Hidden Negatives inside a phrase?

Instead, consider using Clear Positives. They acknowledge and elevate everyone in the conversation and honor their point of view which, in turn, helps establish trust.

> **Lose:** Let's see if we can't find a compromise.
> *This implies that you can't do something, like compromise, because the other person is difficult.*
> **Use:** Let's see if we can find a compromise.
> **Use:** Let's find a compromise.
>
> **Lose:** I don't disagree, but my point is . . .
> *This implies that I don't really disagree with them, but what I'm about to say is way more important.*
> **Use:** I agree . . . and I would add . . .
> I hear you . . . and I also think . . .
>
> **Lose:** You're not wrong. The supply chain is a mess.
> *This implies that I don't think they're really wrong, but I'm still more right than they are.*
> **Use:** You're right. The supply chain is a mess. And I also believe that . . .
>
> **Lose:** I would argue that
> *This implies that we need to argue to have this conversation. Certainly, in a courtroom and some other*

circumstances it is necessary to argue. Not necessarily in other situations.

Use: I feel strongly about
I would debate that
I would contend that
I would reason that
I would dispute that
I would affirm that
I would assert that
I would advocate, urge, press for

Lose: I'll fight for this project.
This implies that we can only come to a conclusion or win with a knock-down, drag-out fight.

Use: I'll champion this project
I'll go to bat for
I'll do everything I can
I'm laser-focused on
I'll commit to
I'll work hard for
I'll advocate, endorse, support, back, promote

You may notice that I am passionate about losing the words argue and fight. I believe there is too much arguing and fighting in the world, and it's not always necessary. Instead, whenever possible, let your language promote positive action and outcomes.

Flip couldn't & can't into can

Lose: I couldn't agree more.
Use: I agree with you.
I agree 100%.
You are spot on!

Lose: I couldn't be more proud of our team.
Use: I am immensely proud of our team. Thank you all.

Lose: I can't thank you enough.

Use: Thank you from everyone in our department.
A huge thank you to everybody.
A heartfelt thank you. Your skills and dedication to complete this project on schedule made all the difference in our success.

"Is 'Right?' Where It's 'At'?"

Although many conversations in the U.S. are crammed with Fillers, Hedges, and Validators, one word is the trifecta, "right?"

In recent years, I've noticed people lift their voice and repeatedly say "right?" in the middle of or at the end of their sentences. It's similar to the Canadian "eh?" or the French, "n'est-ce pas?" meaning, "Correct, is it not?" In the U.S., using the word right (with a question mark) makes it seem as if the speaker wants us to validate what they're saying without pausing for us to confirm it, right? It's more of a punctuation mark than a question. And it's definitely inspired by popular culture. Plus, it doesn't give others the chance to agree or disagree.[14] It's better to pause and only use "right?" when you need an answer. You'll sound less trendy and more confident.

Speaking of words used at the end of a sentence, let's talk about the word "at." Language is living, and it changes over time. For example, we no longer say, "How art thou?" Today, in some cultures, the preposition "at" tacked on to the end of a sentence is an accepted practice. However, most high school English teachers cringe when they hear a preposition ending a sentence like this: "What's the best number to call you at?" The Grammarly blog writes that ending a sentence with "at" is less formal but not incorrect for emails or texts to friends.[15] It's even included in the Gmail autocomplete feature.

- Where are we meeting at?

- Where are you working at?

- Where is the file at?

- On that issue, here's where I'm at.

"At" is a necessary word, but in my view, "at" used at the end of a sentence doesn't communicate professional presence. Grammarly suggests that in business situations, whether it's a proposal, pitch, or presentation, either in writing or in a conversation, it's best to avoid ending sentences with prepositions, like "at."[16]

The simple fix is to drop it from the end.

- What's the best number to call you?
- Where are we meeting?
- Where are you working these days?
- Where is the file, please?
- On that issue, here's where I am. Or, on that issue, here's where I stand.

Grammar | Pronoun Bonus: Me, Myself, and I.

Misusing the pronouns "me," "myself," and "I" are grammatical mistakes that are pervasive in our casual culture, even in business.

How often have you heard someone say, "Me and Daniela are working on the proposal?" There are two errors here. The first mistake is referencing yourself before the other person. The second is an incorrect use of the pronoun "me."

Here's how you fix it. Drop the name of the other person and hear how it sounds. For instance, you wouldn't say, "*Me* is working on the proposal." You'd say, "*I* am working on the proposal." Then add the name of the other person first. "*Daniela and I* are working on the proposal." Honor the other person and use *their* name *first*.

Here's another example. "Please give the report to Amir and I to review." Again, drop the name of the other person and hear how it sounds. You wouldn't say, "Please give the report to *I* to review." Instead, you'd say, "Please give the report to *me* to review." The correct sentence is "Please give the report to *Amir and me* to review."

What about, "Please contact myself or my colleague, Chip if you have any questions." Once again, drop the name of the other person and hear how it sounds. You wouldn't say, "Please contact *myself* if you have any questions." Instead, you'd say, "Please contact *me* if you have any questions." The correct sentence is, "Please contact *my colleague Chip or me* if you have any questions." Like the other two examples, this sentence honors the other person by using *their* name *first*.

Tip: "Myself" is always paired with the pronoun "I" and involves something you do to yourself. For instance, "I thought to myself, if anyone has any questions, I hope they contact my colleague Chip or me."

No one will ever be distracted when you use correct grammar, but they may be distracted if you make grammatical errors. Think of good grammar as a gift to the listener to help them focus what you're saying, not on a grammatical faux pas. Plus, good grammar enhances your professional presence.

Third-Party Proof

In most professions, we are selling ourselves or our organization's products and expertise to develop relationships, attract clients, and build business. As an ambitious professional, you also want to advance your career. But you may be uncomfortable bragging about yourself or promoting your company. So let others do it for you. Use testimonial language—third-party proof—to establish your company's capabilities and your own credentials. It's a good way to build your confidence without overtly "bragging."

- I'm known as the manager who trains people so well that . . .

- My last client said that being a quick learner is my superpower!

- Here's what sets our services/our team/our company apart.

- Our strategic partners say that our strength is . . .

- Industry experts know our company as the leader in . . . What we'd also like you to know is . . .

- We're known as the firm/company/organization that . . .

- Our most satisfied clients say . . .

- Our most successful customers will tell you . . .

Comb through your company's website and your own LinkedIn profile. Both should be ripe with Words to USE to promote your organization and you.

Every 30 days.
It can take 30 days to break a bad habit or form a good one. There are plenty of lists of Words to LOSE and Words to USE in this book. If you try to be aware of all of them, you may get overwhelmed. Instead, give yourself 30

days to LOSE one word or phrase and another 30 days to USE one word or phrase. Be patient with yourself, knowing that with time and practice, your Words to USE will become second nature, like building a muscle, and that builds confidence.

> "The words you speak become the house you live in."
> — Hafiz

Coarse, Crude, Foul Language

If you find yourself cussing more or hearing people using crude language, "Blame the #%$ Pandemic." So reports Anne Marie Chaker in her *Wall Street Journal* article.[17] She highlights the language lowlights that have exploded after we were pushed into the pandemic.

Our work-home boundaries are porous. We're still Zooming in gym shorts and yoga pants, and our kids and cats are making cameos. Our interactions have become more casual, too. We've let our guard down. And evidently our filters as well. Michael Adams is a linguist who says that pandemic stress, blurred boundaries, and exhaustion make it "a perfect swearing storm."[18]

You might be thinking, "I cuss to get people's attention" or "I'm just being myself." I hear you. We all want to be ourselves. But we also need to respect that other people may be offended by expletives.

You might also be thinking, "It's not a problem for me. I can code-switch and stop myself from cussing when I'm with people who I think won't like it." In my experience, it's tricky to toggle between cussing and using more refined language. Plus, you never really know who will be okay with it and who will be offended. It's risky.

Remember the key Confidence Project tenet from Chapter 3: It's easier to go from professional to casual than from casual to professional. Once people see you and hear how you present yourself, it's hard for them to think of you differently the next time. In the case of cussing, err on the side of professional.

"Ok, You Guys. Let's Get Started."

Whenever I hear someone say, "you guys," I think, "I'm not a guy." And it's not only men who say it. For several years, I've attended a well-established, highly regarded women's leadership group, and the founder consistently says,

- "Thanks for being here, you guys."
- "What do you guys think about . . .?"
- "I'm impressed with the work you guys are doing."

Clearly, "you guys" is embedded in popular culture, but unless you're in a college fraternity or a duck blind with your bros,

Lose: You guys
Use: You all   People
         You two   Folks
         Everyone   Colleagues
         Everybody here   Humans
         Team   Friends

Look at all your options. Be creative, you guys. No! Be creative, everybody!

Decide.

One afternoon, my friend Mary and her 30-something daughter Maddie were having a visit. As Maddie was leaving, Mary asked her, "May I give you some feedback on something I heard you say several times today?"

Maddie reluctantly said, "OK."

"I heard you say, 'you know' a lot."

Maddie paused and nonchalantly said, "I did? Oh, OK. Good to know. Bye, Mom."

A few weeks later when Maddie visited again, Mary noticed that she didn't say, "you know." Not one time. After a while Mary said, "Maddie, I haven't heard you say, 'you know.' How did you lose it?" Maddie smiled. "I decided!"

You can decide, too.

CHAPTER 7

The NOW Apology

Have you noticed people apologizing in a variety of circumstances for any number of reasons? Do you reflexively say, "I'm sorry" in emails and conversations? If you're Siri, you get to apologize. "Sorry, I didn't catch that. Could you try again?" Or "Sorry, I can only search by topic for Movies!" Unlike Siri, we humans need to be careful not to over-apologize. These days, "I'm sorry" has become so overused and misappropriated that it has a name, The Sorry Syndrome, and there's a book to go with it by John Waterhouse.[1]

There are many reasons why people apologize. You want to seem nice, more likable, less aggressive. You want to avoid confrontation. Or it could be an unconscious habit. There's a downside to over-apologizing, though. It chips away at your confidence. It sends a message that you're making all kinds of mistakes when you're not. And constantly saying "I'm sorry" is exhausting for you and everyone around you. Plus, when you over-apologize you could be overlooked for a promotion or an opportunity. Others may not see you as having leadership potential.

To complicate the sorry situation, the word sorry has more than one context. Therefore, there are times when sorry *is* the Word to USE.

Cultural Context. In cultures such as the U.K., Australia, and New Zealand, if someone misses a comment, it's common to hear "Sorry?" It's not so much an apology as it is, "I missed what you said, would you kindly repeat it?" Once at a Confidence Project seminar, someone raised their hand with a big grin. "I'm from Canada. We apologize all the time!" The crowd laughed! When I was presenting to a group in London, one fellow said, "We Brits are a proper lot. Someone bumps into *us* and *we* apologize!" More laughter! If you're working cross-culturally, be mindful of differing norms.

Admit Mistakes. When you've made a mistake or there's a misunderstanding, absolutely apologize. It takes courage and confidence to do so because it feels vulnerable. Yet, a sincere apology is vital to build or rebuild trust. "I'm sorry I missed the deadline. I know that threw off your project calendar. I am committed to getting the information to you by end of the day on the 23rd. Will that date work for you?"

Express Empathy. As the world deals with compounding crises, we need expressions of empathy more than ever. It can be as simple as saying, "I'm sorry you're going through this situation. What do you need me to know? What can I do to support you? How can I help you?"

Here's the Confidence Project method for a sincere apology.

1. Name your mistake
2. Apologize
3. Make good on it
4. Move on

For example:

1. I interrupted you when you were leading the all-hands.
2. I'm sorry for overstepping my bounds.
3. Next time, I'll remember to pause before jumping in.
4. You did a great job running the event.

Note: During your apology, be willing to listen and respond to the other person.

The Now Apology

While some "I'm sorrys" are justified, think about your own conversations or group discussions and notice how often you hear or say, "I'm sorry." If you find yourself over-apologizing, consider this simple solution: shift from saying "I'm sorry" to "thank you." As I tell my clients, "Thank you is the Confident NOW Apology."

In Person or Online

Lose: I'm sorry you seem upset.
> *Unless it's your error, or you inadvertently embarrassed or offended someone, or you stepped on their toe, you don't need to apologize for other people's feelings.*

Use: It looks like you're upset, Leo. How can I help?

Lose: I'm sorry to ask this question, but . . .
> *Questions are good. They demonstrate curiosity. CEOs say they look for people with a high CQ (Curiosity Quotient).*

Use: I have a question about that.
I have a clarifying question, please.
Is now a good time for questions?

Lose: I'm sorry, I don't understand. Or Sorry, I don't get it.
> *When you say you don't understand or don't get it, it may seem as if you're not smart. You are. Instead, the person who's delivering the message may not be clear. And if you don't understand, chances are other people don't either.*

Use: Would you clarify that point, please?
Would you say more, please?
Could you expand on that idea, please?
Would you focus-in on that 2nd point?
Walk us through that last point, please?

Lose: I'm sorry, I don't know the answer.
You don't need to know all the answers, but you can research and respond later or ask for a re-frame.

Use: I don't know the answer, but I can get it to you by Monday. How does that work for you?

I want to add some insight, but I need you to rephrase your question, so I'm sure I understand it correctly.

Lose: I'm sorry, I disagree.
Everyone is entitled to their own opinion and should feel encouraged to voice it in meetings or conversations. Trust the richness of your perspective.

Use: I respectfully disagree.
I have a different opinion.
I have another perspective.
I have an alternate position.
Here's how I see it.

Lose: I'm sorry. I've changed my mind.
Give yourself permission to change your mind. And extend that option to others. Conditions and priorities change. You get new information. Time and experience

give you fresh insights. Have the courage to change your mind and speak it.

Use: I've changed my mind. Here's where I am now.

I've changed my mind. I have new information. Here's what I'm thinking.

If English is not your first language, no need to apologize. Instead, consider saying,

"As you can hear, English is not my first language. Thank you for your patience with my accent and the way I express myself. If you need me to clarify anything, please let me know."

Continue with confidence.

Lose: I'm sorry. I'm not used to criticism.
Receiving "constructive criticism" rarely feels constructive. We gravitate toward the negative. Hold back the negative and consider the totality of your good work.
Use: Thank you for your feedback. That's good insight for me. I'll reflect on it.

Lose: Sorry, I blew it.
It may not be as bad as you think.

Use: Thanks for pointing that out. Do you have any other suggestions on how I can improve? I want to make it right.

Lose: Sorry for taking up your time.
We all have value. We all have 24 hours in a day. Your time is as valuable as everyone else's.

Use: Thank you for the opportunity to present my proposal. I appreciate your interest.

Thanks for a great conversation. Let's keep in touch on LinkedIn.

Thank you for the interview. Do you have any final questions for me/us?

Lose: Sorry, do you have a second?
A "second" indicates that the topic is insignificant. And it's not truthful. Almost nothing takes one second to say. Even if you can say it in a few seconds, be prepared for a longer conversation later, if the other person only has a short time to listen right now.

Use: Is now a good time to talk?

"Do you have 5 minutes to talk right now?" *If they don't, ask,* "When is a good time?"

Two people heading for one door at the same time:

Lose: I'm sorry.
Manners still matter. Be polite and offer people the go-ahead, especially if they seem agitated or in a hurry.

Use: After you
Go ahead.
If you are in a hurry, use your "I Statement."

Use: I have a meeting that starts in a few minutes. May I go ahead of you, please? Thanks very much.

Email

Business emails should be brief, clear, and indicate any separate attachments. With 200 emails a day, you don't want yours to be labeled TLDR, Too Long. Didn't Read.

Lose: I'm sorry, I'm late responding to your email.
Use: Thank you for your patience. I've taken a few days to think through my response.

Thank you for waiting. I wanted to collect (or review) the data before getting back with you.

Thank you for your patience. I'm catching up on my unanswered emails today.

I missed your email until now. Thanks for the reminder.

I missed your email until now. Thanks for waiting for my reply.

Texts

Lose: I'm sorry I didn't respond right away. I saw your text but forgot to reply.

Sorry I didn't text you back. I started to answer, then forgot to finish it.

Use: *Replies similar to emails.*

Thank you for your patience.

Thanks for waiting.

Thanks for understanding.

Thank you for the reminder.

There's an app for that!

The "Just Not Sorry" app is a Google chrome extension that highlights keywords and phrases that can undermine your point.[2] For example:

Hey Citlalli,

Sorry to take so long getting back to you.

I'm just writing to say that I'm a little concerned that the 30 minutes allotted for the sales proposal might be kind of short, but I'm pretty sure we can trim the content.

Let's discuss at our meeting tomorrow.

Thanks,
Lou

Here's a stronger email with Words to USE that removes "I'm sorry" and other Words to LOSE that Google might miss.

Note: I changed "Hey" to "Hi" because I believe Hey is too casual for a business email, especially if you don't know the person well.

> Hi Citlalli,
>
> Thank you for your patience as our team prepares the sales proposal for the client meeting on August 25th.
>
> I'm concerned that the 30 minutes allotted to present the proposal is too short. I'm confident, however, that we can trim the content, so we'll have time for questions.
>
> Let's discuss at our final prep meeting at your office on August 22nd at 1 p.m. ET.
>
> Thanks,
> Lou

Before you press send, catch your "sorrys" and other Words to LOSE and replace them with Words to USE. That helps build confidence.

And Then Came 2020

Beginning in 2020, when we were thrust into the pandemic, and WFH with non-stop video calls, people started uttering more "I'm sorrys" than ever.

Video Calls

> **Lose:** Sorry, I'm late for the call.
> **Use:** Thanks for your patience.
>   Thanks for waiting for me.

The NOW Apology

Lose: Sorry, I was on mute.
Use: Thanks for the reminder. *(to unmute)*
   Or as one of my clients says with a grin, "Thanks for letting me know. I was rehearsing!"

Lose: Sorry. Can you hear me?
Use: Thanks for letting me know if you can hear me.

Lose: Sorry. I'm having Wi-Fi issues.
Use: Thanks for understanding my internet situation.

Lose: Sorry, my camera isn't working for some reason.
Use: Thanks for being flexible. My camera isn't working today. (Tech support is on the way.)

Lose: Sorry, you cut out. Can you repeat that?
Use: Would you repeat that, please? You cut out for a moment.

Lose: Sorry for the noise. It's my neighbor's leaf blower.
Use: Thanks for your patience with the noise.

Lose: Sorry. The crazy cat!
Use: Thanks for welcoming my cat!

Lose: Sorry, the babysitter is late.
Use: My daughter wants to say, "Hello!"
   Please meet Andy, my junior assistant!

Lose: (With the half-second delay) Sorry to interrupt.
Use: After you, *or* Go ahead, please.

WFH

Lose: Sorry, this room is a mess.

Use: Thanks for ignoring my background. I'm sharing a home office.

Better yet, blur your background and don't mention the clutter.

Lose: Sorry, my child's crying, dog's barking, doorbell's ringing . . .

Use: Thanks for understanding my family, pet, home life.

Lose: Sorry. I have to use the restroom.

Use: Could you give me a few moments, please? I'll be right back to you. (Click "Stop Video" and mute your mic.) *When you return, say,* "Thanks for waiting."

Lose: Sorry. I haven't eaten all day. I need to grab a quick bite.

Use: Thanks for the break to eat lunch.

Voicemail

Lose: Sorry I'm not here to take your call. Please leave a message and I'll call you back.

Use: Thanks for calling. Please leave a message and I'll call you back.

Out of Office

Lose: Sorry, I'm out of the office through October 11th with limited internet access . . .

Use: Thank you for your email. I value your correspondence and will respond to you when I am back at my desk on October 12th.

More casually. Hello and welcome to my inbox! I am out of the office and will return on October 12th. If you need immediate assistance, please contact _____. Otherwise, I'll reply to your email when I'm back at my desk. Thank you.

With Errors

- Thanks for noting that error, Farzan. I will correct it in the next draft.
- Thank you for bringing this discrepancy to our attention, Rajiv. We will call the vendor right away to address the issue.
- Thanks for flagging, Abby. I'll make the changes.
- Good catch, Ian. I'll make the updates.

RSVPs

Lose: Sorry I'm not able to join you.
Use: Thanks for the invitation. I'm fully committed that day. I appreciate your understanding and hope you have a great event.

A "shelfie"
To practice for an interview, presentation, or critical meeting, prop up your smart phone on a bookshelf and press record. When you listen back, you'll likely hear "sorry" and other Words to LOSE from Chapter 6. It's humbling and illuminating.

Keep calm and carry on. You're the only person listening!

The NOW In Person Shift from "I'm Sorry" to "Thank You"

Lose: Sorry, I'm not shaking hands.
Use: Thanks for introducing yourself. I'm not ready to shake hands yet, but it's good to meet you in person.

Lose: Sorry. We're standing too close.
Use: Let's keep our distance. Thanks.

Heading into a Limited Capacity Elevator

Lose: Oh, sorry.
Use: Thanks for making room. *Or, if there are too many people waiting, say either,* "You go ahead." *or* "May I go ahead, please? I have a conference call shortly. Thanks very much."

If You're Interrupted

Lose: Sorry to interrupt. I just want to say really fast . . .
Use: "I Statements" + A Name

It's easy to default to "I'm sorry" when we get interrupted, especially when the person is a "serial interrupter." We all know one. You might even be one and not know it.

James Mills was the hard driving co-founder and CEO of Medline Industries, Inc., a $13B hospital supply company in Illinois. Mr. Mills was famous for wearing powder blue, purple, and red suits and for interrupting. His *Wall Street Journal* obituary states, "During one meeting, when a colleague tried to cut into one of his free-flowing arguments, Mr. Mills said: 'You can interrupt me when I finish.'"[3]

If there's a serial interrupter in your meeting or if you are getting talked over, hold up your hand to signal that you heard the person. Most times, you can have a pleasant facial expression. Then, say their name in a neutral tone. When you say someone's name, it gets their attention and stops them from talking long enough for you to briefly say,

- Liz, hang on a minute, please. You'll be interested in this idea.

- Sean, I'd love to hear your suggestion, but I'd like to finish my thought, please.

- Marc, I'd like to finish sharing my point. Thanks.

- Janelle, I'm almost finished. Then look right back at the group and continue speaking.

Another strategy is called "amplification." It was adopted by the senior women advisors early in the Obama White House. In her *Washington Post* article, Juliet Eilperin writes that the women, "devised a strategy called 'amplification' to hammer across one another's points during meetings. After one woman offered an idea, if it wasn't acknowledged, another woman would repeat it and give her colleague credit for suggesting it."[4]

- I liked Valerie's idea about loosening the timeline to gather more data. Valerie, tell us more about what you're thinking.

- Jake, hold that thought for a moment. Let's hear the rest of Sanjay's idea.

This technique also works well when you want to support any of your co-workers who may be introverted, reserved or simply quiet. When someone starts to talk over them, amplification is a great technique to silence the interrupter.

- Stephanie, I don't want to miss Astead's point. Hang on a second. Go ahead, Astead.

If you can't get a word in edgewise, be patient. When the person finishes their point, step in and say,

- Before we move on, I'd like to get back to Jamar's part of the project. Jamar, fill us in."

Amplification lets each person know that when they speak, people will listen, and that elevates everyone in the room.

Practice asserting yourself in front of a mirror. That way, you can see those unconscious nonverbals, plus your posture, facial expressions, and distracting habits like fidgeting with your hair or adjusting your glasses.

Record yourself. You can hear your word choice and listen to your tone of voice, pace, and pitch—any of which can be misinterpreted as unconfident and can give people a reason to interrupt you.

Posture, tone, and a pleasant facial expression are gender neutral, and can speak confidence for you.

If You Want to Interject

Lose: Sorry, can I jump in here? I just have a quick comment.

Use: "I" Statements + Acknowledge + A Name
- Debi, I can weigh in on that.
- Bryan, I'll offer this.
- I'll tag on to Jesse's comment.
- Rishad, good point. I'll add this.
- Evie, I like where you're going. Here's my thought.
- Bruno, I can see what you're saying. I have another perspective.

- Adamari, I hear you. However, on our team . . .

Don't apologize. Don't dwell. Carry on with confidence.

If someone derails the discussion, consider taking the lead and

> **Use:** Let's get back on track. The budget is our next agenda item.
>
> We need to cover other critical issues, so let's move on, please.
>
> In the interest of time and everyone's schedules, let's jump to our next topic.

Remember, Words to LOSE including "I'm sorry" are not wrong, and they don't need to be banned for life. Simply be mindful of misusing or overusing them. Instead, when you're tempted with Words to LOSE from Chapter 6 or any of the "I'm sorrys," in this chapter, pause, breathe, and trust.

Pause to gather your thoughts.

Breathe. Voice coach Linda Brice says, "Breathing consciously is the key to getting your voice to flow out of you like a river. When the breath begins to flow again, the thoughts flow too, and those Words to LOSE will disappear."[5]

Trust that the words you choose will be clear, effective, and influential. As Linda Brice told me, "The way we communicate is a direct tool for leadership and change."[6]

People will listen.

CHAPTER 8

Own Your Name + Honor Others

> *"Remember that a person's name is to that person the sweetest and most important sound in any language."*
> – DALE CARNEGIE

As a news reporter, I interviewed CEOs & senators, rock stars & movie stars, moms & dads, and kids & crooks. This I know for sure: we each own four, essential identity markers.

1. Our reputation—What other people think of us, based on how we present ourselves in person and online.

2. **Our character**—The alignment of what we do when no one is watching and what we stand for when everyone is watching.

   3. **Our story**—The verbal and emotional narrative that describes how we arrived where we are in life today.

   4. **Our name**—Our name is fundamental to our personal and professional identity. And, I believe, unless you've achieved mononym status like Adele, Beyoncé, or Sting, most successful people introduce themselves using their first and last names. Own yours.

Shortly after Congressman John Lewis passed away on July 17, 2020, I heard a rebroadcast of an interview he gave on Martin Luther King Day in 2009.

Lewis said when he met Martin Luther King, Jr., Dr. King asked him, "Are you John Lewis?" Lewis, only 18 years old, answered, "Dr. King, I am John Robert Lewis. I gave my whole name."[1]

Use People's Names

Given the pandemic and upheaval we've all faced, there's never been a better time to make people feel seen, heard, valued, included, and honored for their heritage by using their name. Hearing your own name activates a part of your brain that gets your attention, something Dr. Dennis Carmody and

Morgan Lewis found when conducting a study that used a functional MRI. Hearing their own names said aloud holds children's attention long enough that they become self-aware and able to respond and react to the names of others.[2]

This research demonstrates that we are hard-wired from an early age to not only respond to our own name, but that hearing our name creates the opportunity to capture or refocus our attention.

Remembering people's names and using them is an easy habit to practice and it helps you instantly connect with them. Saying someone's name also makes it more likely that they'll remember you. In meetings, intentionally acknowledge co-workers, prospects or clients by name and notice how the energy rises and your conversations flow.

Unusual or Hard to Pronounce Names

In The World of Work now, like at any time, it can rattle your confidence if you can't pronounce someone else's name. In a perfect world, we would receive the names of participants ahead of a meeting. If you're lucky enough to be in that situation, practice the names out loud.

One of my favorite websites is **www.howtopronounce.com**. This is especially helpful when you know in advance who you'll be meeting. For many pronunciations, simply type the name in Search for a Word, click on the green audio triangle, and you can hear the name pronounced. You're often offered a few options, but the common pronunciation comes up first.

I practice like this: tap the audio icon, listen to the pronunciation, and say it aloud.

Tap. Listen. Say it aloud. Repeat this practice until you feel comfortable saying the name. In my experience, once you hear yourself saying a name you're not familiar with, you'll have the auditory memory to pronounce it on cue with confidence.

Honor Your Culture

What if your *own* name is difficult to pronounce? It can be exhausting and embarrassing to constantly correct people. If that happens to you, do you typically let it go and allow people to butcher your name? Don't. Those perpetual mispronunciations can chip away at your confidence. Be proud of your name. Embrace your family heritage and your culture. *And* indulge people with a short mnemonic device to help them pronounce your name the way *you* want.

A few years ago, after I spoke at a business lunch, a woman walked up to me to introduce herself. "I'm happy to meet you," she said. "My name is Shin Chin Yu."

I said, "Hello. Would you say your name again for me, please? I want to get it right."

"Sure!" She grinned and pointed to her shin, her chin, then to me: "Shin—Chin—You." How creative was Shin Chin Yu? No doubt, she has been constantly asked how to pronounce her name. What I'll always remember is her patience and playfulness in helping me to pronounce it correctly.

Note: If you are struggling to pronounce someone's name, you may be tempted to say, "That's a beautiful name." or "I've never heard that name before." Some people whose names are unusual say that those comments can feel "otherizing," making them feel even more different. Better to simply ask, "How do you say your name?" or "Would you say your name again, please? I want to get it right."

If your name is difficult to pronounce, you can add the phonetic spelling in your email signature.

For example: Lucus Delectorskaya (De lec tor *SKY* ya)

Generally, there are no character limits, so you can share your pronunciation and perhaps your preferred pronouns.

For example: Ruqayya (Ru *KAI* ya) Jarad
(she/her/hers)

You can also add the NameCoach link. https://cloud.name-coach.com/. Click on the purple "Hear my name" custom button. Readers will hear *you* pronounce your name and even learn its meaning or the story behind it. NameCoach provides "accurate audio name pronunciations to promote inclusion, belonging, and rapport in every interaction."[3]

On the Phone

If your name tends to trip people up, be proactive when you answer the phone by saying it *first*. If you begin the call with, "Hello. This is, Vikashni," people won't have to guess how to pronounce it. Say it a bit slowly and highlight the accent, as in, "Vi KAASH nee" so your name is clearer for the caller. It's a small courtesy to the other person.

Take a micro-beat between your first and last name. Of course, you know how to pronounce your own name correctly, but people who are meeting you for the first time may not. "My name is Tracy – Hooper."

On Video Calls

Lucky for us, people's names are displayed in the corner of their on-screen image. But that doesn't help us to pronounce their name if it's unusual or complicated.

To avoid awkwardness, especially if you are the call host or leader, log on 5 minutes early, so when people arrive you can ask those with tricky names to pronounce them for you. "Hi, Shefali? Did I pronounce your name right?" After they tell you the correct pronunciation, repeat it to confirm and hear it again. (This gives others on the call a chance to hear it, too.)

Have a paper and pen ready to jot it down and mark it up for visual cues. For instance, I write down names phonetically, then underline, add hyphens, or whatever else helps me to say the name correctly. As in, Shef-ALL'-lee. Like many people, Shefali will be impressed and grateful that you made the effort to get their name right.

Leaders can model confidence by taking that extra moment to ask how to pronounce someone's name. You are sending a message of allyship and inclusion—that everyone belongs on that call, in that meeting, and in that organization.

Name Block In Person

How often have you recognized someone, but you cannot remember their name? And you think, "I hope they don't see *me* see *them*!" Do you dash in the other direction?

Instead, pre-empt. Be mindful of physical distancing when appropriate and walk toward them. If you have a mask on, consider briefly pulling it down so they can recognize you. Smile, give a NOW Hello gesture and say, "Hi. Good to see you. I'm Tracy Hooper." Offering your name *first* generally prompts them to say their name, and you're saved from the embarrassment of not recalling theirs.

That may seem like a lot of work simply to say "Hello" to someone whose name you can't remember! However, after such a long time of limited socializing, WFH, and seeing each other out of context, some people may be slightly confused and also crave human connection. Take heart and be the person who provides the triple threat: Connection. Compassion. Good communication.

If pre-empting doesn't work, and they say *your* name *first*, try one of these phrases.

- "Hi. You look familiar to me. Remind me of your name."

- "Hi there. I remember you from the meeting in Anaheim. Will you help me with your name, please?"

- "Hi. Thanks for remembering my name. Remind me of yours."

You might get caught with the embarrassing reply, "I'm George Andino. We've met five times before!" If that happens, jump back in with, "Oh, you're right, George. We're out of context. Thanks for remembering me. Great to see you again. How are you doing these days?" or "What do you think of the meeting so far?" or "What was your big takeaway from the speaker?"

Don't dwell. Don't make excuses. Don't apologize. Avoid Words to LOSE such as, "Oh, sorry. I'm terrible with names." or "Sorry, I'm good with faces but bad with names." Simply keep the conversation going with confidence.

If you realize you've been mispronouncing someone's name for months (or years!) say this:

> "I've just learned that I've been mispronouncing your name all this time. I see that it's _____. Am I saying it right?" They'll be thrilled. Then, continue right into the conversation.

If someone else has mispronounced *your* name for months (or years!) have a pleasant expression on your face and use a neutral tone with your "I Statement."

> **YOU:** "Since we've known each other for a while (or for some time), I thought you'd want to know that my name is pronounced _____."

Most people will apologize, "I'm sorry! Have I been saying it wrong all these years? Thanks for telling me."

> **YOU:** "Thank you for wanting to get it right. Here's a mnemonic device that helps: _____." Then you can move the conversation along with confidence.

In our global work environment, make it a daily practice to show inclusion and confidence by owning your name and honoring others', too.

CHAPTER 9

The NOW Networking

Networking is as simple as reaching out to someone who shares your same interests whether in person or online. When you respond to a LinkedIn post that a colleague or someone in your industry shared, you're networking. If you ask a friend to refer you to their trusted accountant or business coach, you're networking. When you read the confidence techniques in this chapter, think of them as part of your weekly routine, rather than a daunting, dreaded necessity to expand your career.

Networking can also be more formal. You may not be meeting at a big hotel with crowds of people *yet*, trying to be memorable by passing out business cards, or lifting your lanyard for someone to click your QR contact code. But there are still many effective ways to network naturally and with confidence. Networking, like The World of Work now, is a mindset: it's about building relationships in person or virtually with new people. It's also about realizing how you can maintain connections with colleagues, business leaders, or prospects across your own organization or industry. Still, the feelings associated with networking can range from at ease to mildly uncomfortable to scared stiff.

Does this "self-talk" resonate with you:

- "I'm an introvert and networking isn't my thing."
- "I don't want to sell myself. I want my work to speak for itself."
- "My colleagues or folks at other companies are too busy. Why would they want to make time for me?"
- "I don't want to network internally. I might inconvenience my boss or another leader and waste their time."

Introvert, extrovert, or anywhere in between, you can learn how to network successfully with confidence.

The NOW In-Person Networking

It's clear: in-person networking, trade shows, business meetings, industry summits, leadership retreats, live conventions, and social events have changed. When you arrive, do you need to show proof of vaccination or a negative COVID-19 test? Are masks still required or optional? Are you comfortable shaking hands and hugging again or giving high fives? And those are just a few of the questions to answer before you even start talking with people!

With the pandemic, most in-person networking functions were cancelled. Now, as we learn to live with the virus, live events with real humans are roaring back! Even if the gatherings are outside, or inside with good ventilation, many will have strict protocols for guests to pass a clearance checkpoint. Still, whether you're eager to schmooze again or not, you can learn several smart skills to feel more confident, even if you don't know anyone else in the room.

The Perfect Pair:
Pre-empt the Awkward + "I Statements"

In fall 2021, I was invited to an awards ceremony for a terrific client whose business was named one of the fastest growing private companies in Oregon. I was thrilled for him and cautious about going. It was the first big business event I'd attended in almost two years. I drove with my colleague, Carrie, who proactively and kindly put me at ease when she texted, "On my way to pick you up. I'm OK not wearing a mask in the car with you, but I'm happy to follow your lead."

I replied, using "I Statements," just as Carrie had: "Thanks for the option. I'm covering my lipstick and wearing a mask!" When Carrie arrived, the car windows were down, and her mask was up. By texting ahead of time, she honored my comfort level. That's Pre-empting the Awkward.

There were a few hundred people at the event. Some wearing masks, others not. Lots of folks shook hands like it was 2019, a choice that many people are feeling comfortable with now. I had prepared my own Pre-empt the Awkward strategy. Earlier that day I practiced in front of a mirror. (It may seem hokey, but I wanted to see my facial expression, check my posture, and hear my greeting.) I put my right hand over my chest, smiled and said, "Hi there. I'm not quite ready to shake hands, but I'm glad to meet you in person!" I was primed.

In the moment, though, I got caught off guard. Someone introduced themselves and automatically extended their hand. I hesitated for a half-second but accepted it anyway. I didn't feel great about it. And after the conversation ended, I pumped a drop of Purell from the table and reminded myself, "Practice makes progress."

The following week I attended a networking event. This time, I was more prepared for the various greetings. When someone went in for a handshake, I smiled, tapped my right hand over my heart and said, "Hi Andrea. Good to meet you. I'm not ready to shake hands quite yet." Her reply? "I *totally* get that! Great to meet you, too." As we started talking, I was reminded again how practice, resilience, and courtesy smooth the runway to enjoy new networking opportunities.

Color-coded accessories to signal your boundaries

To Pre-empt the Awkward and help ease the way back to face-to-face greetings and conversations, check out businesses like Elation Factory Co.[1] It offers customers a "Social Distancing Event Kit" that "allows guests to, quite literally, read the room."[2]

It includes display signs and colored-coded wristbands like a traffic light. RED means, "Gonna wave from six feet." YELLOW means, "Okay with talking but no touching." GREEN means, "Okay with hugs, high fives and handshakes."

It's not confusion-free, however. Some people switch colors during an event, as they get more comfortable with the crowd!

Whether networking, attending meetings or reconnecting with your co-workers, it's more important than ever to know your boundaries. Make them clear and quickly tell others what they are. This is especially important with various perspectives about masks, physical greetings, and vaccination status.

Using "I Statements" helps keep conversations friendly rather than cringy or confrontational. They also keep other people from getting defensive. You are not making judgments.

You're simply and kindly stating what actions you're taking without commenting on another person's behavior. In short, "I Statements" are key to keeping conversations calm, civilized and confident. Here are a few examples:

Take the Lead
Build your confidence by being the person who gracefully sets the expectations or precautions *before* in-person meetings. A client used this approach by texting me ahead of our face-to-face appointment: "I'm fully vaccinated, but with the Omicron variant, I think it would be smart to wear masks, just in case. Does that work for you?"

He Pre-empted the Awkward by taking the lead and using "I Statements," so neither of us felt weird in the moment. He clearly stated his boundaries ahead of time, and it was easy to honor his request. When we met in person we were immediately at ease and got right into our conversation without fumbling for masks or awkwardly asking questions.

You can also take the lead and Pre-empt the Awkward with an email or phone call:

- "I'm fully vaccinated, and I would appreciate it if we would both still wear masks. What are your thoughts?"
- "Whether or not either of us is vaccinated, I would appreciate our wearing masks and keeping some distance."

- "I'm fully vaxxed and boosted, so I'm comfortable not wearing a mask when we meet. What do you prefer? Either way is fine with me."

- "I've had COVID and am fully recovered. But I'm happy to wear a mask if you'd like me to."

- "I'm not wearing a mask or distancing, but I'll follow your lead."

Practice these "I Statements" out loud. Once you hear the words come out of your mouth, you'll know you can say them again. That way when you see someone, whether spontaneously or planned, you'll be ready. There are lots of ways to phrase what you're comfortable with, express your wishes, and honor what other people prefer.

Additional "I Statement" Suggestions

These are small requests or statements, but knowing your boundaries and telling people what you want shows confidence and respect for everyone's well-being.

- **Stick to Company Policies:** "Hi. Good to meet you. I'm following our company guidance and keeping some distance. But it's great to finally meet in person. How are you today?"

- **Mask Fatigue:** If someone says, "I am so over masks." Say, "Me too, but I'm still wearing one to stay safe." Or "I hear you. I'm tired of them, too. But for now, I feel more comfortable wearing one."

- **Uncomfortable meeting in person:** "I'd prefer if we meet by Zoom instead of in person. I hope you understand."

- **Respond to an in-person conference invitation:**
  - "Thanks for the invitation. I'm still cautious about being in large groups, so I've decided to attend the conference virtually. I look forward to participating."
  - "Thanks for inviting me to your event. I won't be able to attend this time. I hope it goes very well."

Drop the Apologies + Don't Dwell

There is no need to explain or apologize for your boundaries, as in "Sorry, I'm still wearing a mask." Simply state your request. "I'd like us both to wear masks, please." If someone gets testy or seems annoyed, then they're annoyed. At least they will know where you stand. As always, don't dwell. Simply move ahead with the conversation, showing goodwill and interest in the other person.

Show Respect, Always

If you're comfortable *not* wearing a mask or distancing, don't assume that other people feel the same way. If you go to someone's home, office, or a business meeting and no boundaries were established before getting together, wear a mask. It's a simple, respectful gesture that avoids an awkward greeting. You may find the other person says, "No need to wear a mask." Thank them and start the conversation.

What to wear?
Business Attire. Smart Casual. Informal. Retreat Chic. Black Tie. Black Tie optional. Virtual Meet & Greet. Cocktail +

A seasoned event planner will provide guidance about what is the appropriate dress code, especially if the event has a theme or specific vibe. Good 'ole Google provides endless attire options for different genders, appropriate choices for seasons and weather conditions, clothing suggestions for your role at the event, your industry, after hours gatherings, etc.

If you're unsure about what to wear, look at photos from past events to see what outfits other people have worn.

Know Before You Go Networking

As a TV news reporter, freelance voice-over artist, non-profit fund-raising volunteer, and Founder of The Confidence Project, I have been networking my whole adult life.

Here's what I've found works best:

If you know some people who may be at an event, research to learn more about them. LinkedIn, Instagram, and a Google search work well. Among the various attendees, decide ahead of time the two people you'd like to meet. Not five, ten or fifteen. Two people. If you have time beforehand, email them.

Hi Julie,

I saw your name on the invitation list for the American Marketing Association event next Tuesday. I'll be there too and would like to meet you in person. I admire your innovative work and enjoyed the article you wrote for the Michigan chapter newsletter. Hope to see you next week.

All the best,
– Jarod Abbas

If you know those pre-selected folks slightly or if you're not sure they will be attending, phrase your email this way.

Hi Leigh,

I hope you're having a good week.

I'll be at the Construction Management Association event on Thursday. If you plan to go, I'll look for you there. I appreciate your contributions to the Gulf Coast region and would like to personally thank you.

After a long, dry spell without in-person gatherings, it will be great to reconnect and hear how your business is doing. I hope to see you on Thursday.

Best to you,
– Lorraine Cabrera

LinkedIn recommendations: received *and* given

For the people you're researching, scroll down to the bottom of their LinkedIn page to the Recommendations section. Click on **Received** to see what others have written about them.

For more insight, click on **Given**. Here, you can read the testimonials that the person you're researching offers about *other* people. Their writing will show you what characteristics they find valuable: "Her willingness to jump in." "He never needs prompting." "They make order out of the chaos." Knowing what they admire about others will give you more to talk about and will also make for a more interesting conversation.

Whether or not you know people at the gathering, when you arrive, take a deep breath, and take your time. Get a beverage, wear your Pleasant Resting Face, have your business cards handy or wear the lanyard with your QR contact code. Then start walking. As you move around the room, you may spot someone you've wanted to meet or a person you didn't expect to be there. Great! Be spontaneous and say, "Hello." Otherwise, look for your two key people and have some Kick Starter Questions ready. (See Kick Starters in Chapter 10, Confident Conversations.) These go-to questions can help ease your way into friendly dialogue. You can also practice the Breaking & Entering skills coming up shortly.

When you are in a crowded room, wondering what everyone is talking about, remember, "Everyone's favorite subject is themselves." Therefore, when you approach someone new, ask *them* about *them*. As the conversation continues, be mindful of how long you are talking. In my experience, chatting for about ten minutes makes for a good starter conversation. If you feel that it's going well and they seem engaged, keep going. If you get the sense that they're ready to move on, trust your gut . . . and your eyes. Pay attention. If you notice them glancing around, there's a good chance that their attention is starting to wither. That is your cue to make a graceful, confident exit.

Note: Use The NOW Goodbye Farewell Phrases found in Chapter 11, including some of my personal favorites:

- "I know you want to get around to catch up with some other people, so let's say goodbye for now. Take care."

- "I bet you want to get around to meet some other folks, so I'll let you go. If I don't see you again tonight, good luck with your presentation next week."

- "Before we say goodbye, I'd love to exchange business cards
    - so we can stay connected on LinkedIn."

- *or*, so I can send you the link to that article in Forbes."
- *or*, so I can introduce you to Alexander Lachenmeier."

I love business cards or the digital equivalent. I keep cards in every pocket, purse, and laptop case. If someone gives you their business card, take a moment to look at it. If you've already forgotten their name, it's right there in print! Plus, by glancing at it, you honor the golden rule of The Confidence Project: "Treat everyone as if they are the most important person in the room." At that moment, they are!

Breaking & Entering

As you continue to circulate throughout the room, Breaking & Entering conversations can feel awkward, but it doesn't have to. No matter the safety protocols, you can join in a conversation with confidence. There are two basic kinds of social Breaking & Entering. One is a request, "May I join you?" and the other is an invitation, "Come join us."

"May I Join You?"

To break into a conversation, simply approach and ask, "May I join you?" That's it. No need to apologize with, "Sorry to interrupt." "Sorry, am I butting in?" "Sorry, is this a private conversation?" If you want, you can say, "May I join you? I heard you talking about Alycia's promotion . . .or Hawaii . . . or your favorite whiskey." Most of the time, people will welcome you in. It may feel like you're eavesdropping which can be rude. This is one of those times, however, when it's fine to eavesdrop in order to break into a conversation.

Except . . . Toe-to-Toe Means No

If two people are talking, even with distance, and their eyes are engaged and their feet are pointed directly at one another, that means they do not want to be interrupted.

If someone's foot is turned out to the side, however, and they're gesturing and glancing a bit, those are classic, nonverbal cues that the door is open, and you can enter the conversation with confidence. "May I join you?" Most people will say, "Yes." If they say, "Actually, we're finishing up an important conversation. Could you give us a few minutes?" simply say, "Sure. Thanks for telling me. Take care." And move on. No need to apologize.

"Come Join Us."

The other type of social Breaking & Entering is "Come join us." Here's your chance to be aware of social space and group dynamics. If you see someone on the outside of a group, standing alone, extend your arm to invite them in and say, "Come join us. We were just talking about Geoff's golf game or Pat's new Golden Retriever." This technique welcomes the other person *right* into the conversation.

This skill is important because we all know what it feels like to be left out. No matter how confident we are, if we don't know people in a group, or if we're on the outside looking in, our minds can go right back to middle school when we weren't invited to that birthday party or camping trip or were excluded from the "in" group. *You* become the person who's confident enough to bring people into conversations with a welcoming "Come join us." You'll feel empowered by taking the initiative, and people will remember you for being inclusive.

The What Ifs

What If: You're in a conversation. Someone is on the outside, and you *cannot* remember their name.
Do This: Extend your arm and with your hand, guide them into the group.
Say This: "Hi. Come join us. Do you all know each other?"

Typically, people will volunteer, "No, we don't. I'm Carlos San Luis." And everyone else will automatically say their name, too.

What If: You're in a conversation. Someone is on the outside whose name you *do* remember, but you *cannot* remember the names of all the people you're talking to in the group.
Do This: Extend your arm and with your hand, welcome them into the group.
Say This: "Greg, come join us. Everyone, this is Greg Bayles . . . I'll let you all introduce yourselves." It's as if *you* are doing the group a favor, to let *them* introduce

themselves, when really, *they're* saving *you* from stumbling through introductions and hoping you get it right! Nine out of ten times, people will automatically offer their names!

What If: You are physically in a group conversation, but you're not being included in the discussion. How can you exit that conversation with confidence?

Do This: Check your posture, have a neutral facial expression, then wait for a slight pause.

Say This: "You know, everybody, I'll let you all finish your conversation. Take care." And then walk away with your dignity intact. As film director Ava DuVernay says about Oprah Winfrey, "She does not have to tolerate what does not nourish her."[3] Neither do you.

Share Your Gaze

When you're in a group and you're talking, it's easy to look at one person, especially if you know them or they're using micro-cues like nodding or leaning in to show they're listening to you. But a confident conversationalist gives everyone equal eye contact, making each person feel as if they are essential to the conversation. To get started, practice sharing your gaze in conversations with people you know well. With time, this technique will become more natural.

It didn't take a pandemic for people to feel anxious about networking. Even seasoned professionals sometimes get nervous. But after such a prolonged time of limited in-person interaction, there can be nervousness *and* excitement about gathering face-to-face and re-establishing connections. It doesn't matter why you may feel uneasy networking. By rehearsing these skills you'll reduce your anxiety and establish a rhythm that turns networking into a familiar routine. And, who knows, you might find that networking can be fun!

Networking Online

There are ways to expand your professional connections beyond networking in person. Online networking can be quite powerful.

One of my clients, who's a flourishing entrepreneur, says, "It may surprise you to know that I'm not confident networking in person. So, the silver lining in this shift to connecting by Zoom is that I've met more people and had more meaningful conversations than ever in twenty-five years of business. There are no distractions of food, beverages, and other people interrupting our conversations! On video calls, you can zero in on the person right in front of you. Although we have been isolated off and on, I feel more connected than ever."

The NOW Networking makes it possible to connect with people online or in writing, along with face-to-face. It is freeing when you know how to represent your best self in any one of these ways. No matter the medium, if you're reaching out to new people a couple of times a week, you'll soon be making new connections and expanding your relationships.

The NOW Necessity: LinkedIn

Since March 2020, "LinkedIn has been promoted from obligatory to essential," says Charlotte Cowles in her *New York Times* article.[4] If you want to promote your own work or business, expand your business sphere, or are curious about what jobs are out there, then LinkedIn is The NOW Necessity for online networking. Keep your profile up to date with these simple steps:

- Add a new headshot.

- Stay active in your newsfeed so you'll be noticed. LinkedIn algorithms like users who are regulars. Post links to articles relevant in your industry. Like, comment, and share videos, news articles, and stories from others. It's all about engagement. You don't have to generate new content to be "active" on LinkedIn.

- Update your profile and show your personality. It doesn't have to be as formal as your resume, and it helps make you more memorable.

- Make sure your skills are accurate because they are often used as key search words by recruiters to find candidates.

Cowles highlights two LinkedIn features rolled out since March 2020. One of the tools lets you "record practice interviews online and evaluate your performance. The tool uses A.I. powered feedback to assess how fast you're talking, how many times you use filler words ("um" and "like"), and sensitive phrases to avoid."

Another tool is Career Explorer to "steer members toward new roles that align with their skills but may be in a different Industry or area they hadn't previously considered." This tool can boost your confidence, open a door to new career opportunities, or generate ideas on how to find new customers or clients.

Networking By Email

One key to networking and building relationships virtually is to keep in touch without annoying people. Relationships take time to develop. People are busy. They're distracted. Be patient. Over time, you will build trust, the essential ingredient in any strong, long-term relationship.

Grab 'em with the Subject Line

Let the all-important Subject Line be an attention grabber. A good one makes it more likely that your email will be opened and read. Many of the following Subject Lines work because they include a reference to everyone's *favorite* topic: Themselves!

- Congratulations!

- Thought about you when I . . . read this article, found this link, watched this TED Talk

- This article reminds me of our last conversation

- Thanks to you
- Put the name of someone they know
  - Thanks to Gabe Eliopoulos
  - At the suggestion of Aria Okereke
  - Emma Van Fossan recommended I contact you

Salutation: Heave "Hey"

There are several appropriate ways to greet someone in a business email. "Hi. Hello. Greetings. Good morning. Dear Pauline." The greeting I *don't* use professionally in print or in person is, "Hey." As in, "Hey Justin."

"Hey" is culturally popular. You may even hear a serious journalist on the radio, TV or a podcast greet their guest or colleague with, "Hey Ari." In my view, "Hey Ari" is not polished enough for business. Compare it to professional business attire that we covered in Chapter 3. "It is easier to go from professional to casual than to go from casual to professional. Once people see you a certain way, it's hard for them to see you differently the next time. So, err on the side of professional, at least for the first 'Hello.'"

> *"I didn't have time to write you a short letter, so I wrote you a long one."*
> – Mark Twain

Be Brief

If the average professional receives 304 emails every week, checks their smartphone 150 times a day, and spends 28 hours a week on email, then "brevity is the new unspoken expectation." This is according to Joseph McCormack in his book, *[BRIEF] Make a Bigger Impact by Saying Less*.[5]

Mark Twain's quote in 1871 reminds us that it takes time to edit and perfect your message. McCormack describes email brevity this way: Ask yourself, "Do I write emails that get to the point in five lines or less?" It's not always possible, as you'll see in the samples here, but I encourage you to accept this challenge. You may be surprised how often people will start responding to you.

Networking Email GOLD: Give. Give. Give. Ask.

The Give. Give. Give. Ask. approach takes micro-moments for macro impact. A good "give" is personal and specific, with no expectations. It's also written in your authentic voice. For example, you could sign off professionally with *Sincerely, Best regards, With gratitude,* or more conversationally with *Take care, Peace, Bravo! Kudos! Cheers!*

Over time, if you're a "Giver," and focus on building relationships, then when you need to ask for advice, a favor, a recommendation, a referral, an introduction, an interview, or even a job, people are more likely to say, "Let's talk!"

Here's a "Give"

Whenever I read a newspaper article, watch a TED Talk, or listen to a podcast that makes me think of a prospect, client, or someone in my personal or professional world, I email them with the link.

> **To:** Grant
> **Subject:** Thought about you with this article about co-worker camaraderie
>
> Hi Grant,
>
> I hope you are doing well this week.
>
> I thought about you and our conversation last month when I read this article in the *WSJ*. I remember you sharing your vision of being an authentic leader and the challenges of doing it with a remote team. The article highlights how co-workers can build strong relationships even when everyone is virtual.[6] There are some great, actionable ideas that may help support you and your team.
>
> Best of everything to you and your colleagues.
>
> Kind Regards,
> Frans

Another "Give"

> **To:** Anita
> **Subject:** Congratulations!
>
> Hi Anita,
>
> Congratulations on your promotion!

I remember when you started your career in advertising. What a journey. I admire all that you've accomplished including one of your goals to be an influential leader. Now you are—by growing your team, speaking at conferences, and making an impact way beyond your organization.

Bravo!
Walker McCormick

Another "Give"

"Give" an introduction using The Confidence Project Formula:

- How you know each person

- What you admire or respect about them

- Why you want them to meet each other

Note: Hyperlink the company name and each person's LinkedIn page for easy research.

Hello Pamela and Mike,

I hope all is going well for you. I'd like to introduce you to each other.

Mike, <u>Pamela Neferkará</u> is a past client and friend. She's the founder of <u>Elmira Street Associates</u>. In addition to serving on boards and investing in women owned businesses, Pamela is a trusted and wise mentor of young people as part of the <u>Monday Night Mentorship</u>. I admire her deep commitment to ethical leadership and her calm, steady demeanor that conveys confidence and trust.

Pamela, <u>Mike Tarbell</u> is the President of <u>Playbooks Consulting</u>. Mike is an expert in talent management and coaches top executives and their teams to help them reach their full potential. As you know well, key to planning succession is to identify emerging talent deep in the organization for future leadership roles. I have collaborated with Mike on several projects and admire his commitment to mentoring and developing up-and-coming and diverse talent.

I believe the work you are both doing is complementary and I thought you'd benefit from meeting each other to share insights and ideas.

I'll leave you two to connect.

All the best,
Tracy

Spare My Inbox

If Pamela replies first, she'll press "reply all," move me to BCC, and move Mike to the To line. This makes it easier for Mike and Pamela to directly connect.

In her reply, she may say,

> "Tracy, thank you for your generous introduction of Mike and me. I'm moving you to BCC to spare your inbox."
>
> Peace,
> Pamela

Now Pamela and Mike can correspond, and I am out of the loop.

The NOW Networking

Handwrite an Actual Note

Most people get bills and junk mailers in their mailbox. A handwritten note is gold. I love cutting out newspaper and magazine articles, or even a *New Yorker* cartoon or "Pepper & Salt" from the *Wall Street Journal*. I jot a note on Confidence Project letterhead and pop it in the mail. Over the years, countless "thank you" emails have landed in my inbox within 24 hours after someone receives this simple "give."

"It keeps me from looking at my phone every two seconds."

"Tracy,

Thanks for the note. I appreciate you thinking of me. Great cartoon! Hope all's well with you."

A Heartfelt Thank You Note

Dear Steve,

I hope you're doing well this Thursday afternoon.

As this quarter comes to a close, I want to thank you for being a champion of our company. Your generous business referrals have led to several new clients which have resulted in significant business for us. The circle keeps getting bigger thanks to you.

I know you have a demanding schedule and for you to extend yourself to recommend our company is meaningful to me. Thank you for trusting in the work that we do. If there is a way for me to support your business, please let me know. It will be my pleasure.

All the best in Q3,
Patrick Concannon

Send the same email twice

If you send an email to someone and you don't hear back in 10-14 business days, send the exact same email again. If it's time sensitive or date specific, update the change accordingly. In my experience, most people reply quickly, "Thanks for emailing me again. I forgot to respond. *Or* I opened your email and then got distracted. *Or* I meant to get back with you."

Use this technique sparingly. There's a difference between sending a gentle reminder and becoming a pest.

Other Ways to "Give"

- Remember birthdays and work anniversaries.

- Congratulate someone for their new job or new baby.

- Acknowledge a civic recognition, winning a big case, or making an acquisition.

  - Milestones are frequently noted on LinkedIn, in local newspapers, and on TV.

Loss & empathy

In the course of every life and career, there is loss. Loss of a loved one. Loss of health. Loss of a job. The list is long. It may feel awkward, but it is a generous gift to another person when you acknowledge their loss or struggle. Simply send an email, text, or a handwritten card.

> Hi Nancy,
>
> I am thinking about you during this tough time, *or* sad time, *or* challenging time. I wish you well *or* I'm so sorry about . . . *or* I'm sending you thoughts of peace. No need to reply.
>
> Take good care of yourself,
> Richard

By adding, "No need to reply," you relieve the other person of feeling obligated to respond. And that's a gift.

Leaders: Become an "Encourager in Chief"

When Steven Sondheim died on November 26, 2021, at age 91, "the American stage lost not only a composer and lyricist nonpareil but also its long-time encourager in chief,"[7] writes Laura Collins-Hughes.

Sondheim was beloved as a mentor, teacher, and audience regular. He was also a prolific note writer. Collins-Hughes writes, "After Sondheim died, Twitter was flooded with images of them. Notes to students and professionals and fans, they were thoughtful and specific, full of gratitude and good wishes, each on letterhead, each with the elegant, sloping signature that's familiar now from the Stephen Sondheim Theater marquee."

> "June 1, 2004
>
> Dear Lynn Nottage –
>
> I saw your wonderful play last week. It reminded me of why I wanted to write for the theater in the first place.
>
> Thank you and congratulations.
>
> Yours sincerely,
> Stephen Sondheim"

As a leader, you can be as generous and encouraging as Sondheim. Imagine the surprise and delight of your teammates or a client when they receive a generous, handwritten note from you—on your letterhead! (Don't have your own letterhead? Design and order it. It can be reasonably priced and makes a big impact.)

> April 29, 2022
>
> Dear Darius,
>
> Great job on your finalist presentation. You were well prepared, engaged the client, and elevated our team. Thanks a million.
>
> Kudos,
> Your signature

This small "give" can make someone feel valued, boost their confidence, and motivate them to keep going. Plus, it can reinforce your organization's culture and reputation that everyone matters.

Now, Here's an "Ask"

Don't let the fear of asking or the other person's *perceived* status (CEO, president, boss, influencer) become a barrier to networking. Most people *love* to help others or talk about their own career journey. They often want to give advice, give encouragement, and give back.

An Introduction

Dear Rafael,

I hope you're doing well this week.

I noticed on LinkedIn that you know Apoorvah Nooyi. I admire her work and would like to explore collaborating on future projects. Since you and I have worked together, I wonder if you would be willing to make a virtual introduction between Apoorvah and me. It can be as simple as,

> Arno Dlamini and I have worked together with success on several projects. With both of you leading virtual teams and moving towards a hybrid return-to-office model, I thought you would enjoy meeting each other, sharing ideas, and could benefit from collaborating.

Rafael, if making this introduction fits into your schedule, I'd appreciate it. Please know that "yes, no, and not now" are all good answers.

Thanks for your consideration.

Sincerely,
Arno Dlamini

Note: Make your request easy by offering "sample" language. This saves the person time and lets them know exactly why you're asking for the introduction. The result: they are more likely to say "Yes" and respond in a timely manner.

An "Ask" for Advice and Informational Meeting

Dear Yìchén,

I hope your week is off to a good start.

I have been in the IT department for 5 years with several advances and increased responsibility. Like many people today, I am at a career crossroads. I'm considering three different potential next steps. Knowing that everyone's journey is different, I'd like to share these options with you and get your advice because I have always admired you and your stellar reputation in our industry.

Would you be willing to explore these key questions?

1. My next goal is to be a manager, and I haven't had the opportunity to manage a team yet. How do you recommend I get management experience?

2. Early on, how did you tell your story so leaders would listen to you and give you advancement opportunities?

3. Your career path has been nontraditional. If I explore a different career, would you be willing to share how you navigated your journey without a linear path?

I know you have a demanding calendar. If you have time in the next 30-60 days for a 30-minute Virtual Coffee by Zoom, I'll work my schedule around yours. Please know that "yes, no, and not now' are all good answers. Thanks very much.

All best to you,
Yamiche Johansson

Note:
- Sharing your possible next steps or long-term goals clarifies your "Ask" and helps the person on the receiving end to prepare for the meeting.

- Stick to that 30-minute assurance. At 25 minutes say, "I promised we'd be finished in 30 minutes, and I want to respect our time. We have 5 minutes left. Is there any other advice you'd like to share?"

- Finally, a personal, hand-written Thank You note is a must.

(See sample Thank Yous coming up in this Chapter: Gratitude is Always in Style.)

Circle back soon

If someone has made the effort to offer you advice or introduce or recommend you to another person, let them know the outcome. Schedule a calendar event to remind you to circle back.

- "I want to update you on my meeting with Lesley Sluneckova. Thanks to your generous introduction, we are . . . or we have decided to . . . or Lesley connected me with . . . or I took your great advice and . , ,"

It's polite to say, "Thank you" in the moment. It makes a bigger impact to follow up. The person will be delighted to know how their actions or advice made a difference for you. And they'll remember you for it.

Every conversation is an interview.

It's true. You never know where the next job, promotion, recommendation, mentor, sponsor, or career opportunity will come from: a networking event, industry summit, holiday party, neighborhood bar-b-q, virtual conference call, an all-hands, wedding reception, college reunion, on-boarding or training session, a social media connect, a yoga, painting, or writing retreat, at your child's playground, waiting at the start of a half marathon, or in the Delta Airlines queue.

Remember: You take yourself wherever you go. Be the person you'd like to meet and know that every conversation is an interview.

Gratitude is Always in Style

Whenever someone has been generous or kind to you, acknowledge them with a fulsome Thank You.

Hi (name),

- It was a pleasure to meet you at the convention *or*, on October 25th.

- I enjoyed our conversation about your business *or*, thanks for sharing your perspective, *or* offering advice about possible next steps, *or* explaining the market as you see it, *or* offering to introduce me to Anthony Del Vecchio . . .

- Here's what I learned from you. *Or*, I'll remember your advice about that issue. *Or*, I appreciate having the background about . . . *Or*, I appreciate your perspective. (Offer 1-2 sentences of explanation.)

- I look forward to keeping in touch. *Or*, I'll be back in touch when I have an update for you. *Or*, expect my email introduction for you and Melinda Moore next week. *Or*, I'll let you know when Michael and I connect.

- Sincerely, Best regards, Kind regards, Warm regards, All the best, My very best, or Best to you. Consider using the person's name again, as in, Best to you, Leno.

Yes. No. Not now.
In several chapters, I've used the phrase "yes, no, or not now." I learned this gracious line from Alice Tang. Alice

is a top financial advisor. She's also a master networker who regularly hosts virtual and in-person financial seminars for clients and prospects. Over the years, to encourage people to respond to her invitations, she's learned the magic RSVP words. "Yes and no are both good answers." For example, "We hope you can join us on April 12th from 5-7 p.m. at The Heathman Hotel. Yes and no are both good answers."

If you're hoping to meet with a prospective client and you offer several dates for a Virtual Coffee by Zoom, you can end your email in a similar way. For example, "Kindly let me know if one of these dates works for you. And please know that yes, no, and not now are all good answers."

You'll be amazed how quickly people will reply because you've given them an "out" if they can't or don't want to join you. When it's a "No" or "Not Now," you can move on to other prospects and focus your time and energy where you will be more productive.

The Best Business Advice I Ever Got: "I Don't Want to Miss the Chance"

When I was moving along in my TV news career, I was looking for a reporter's job. I landed an interview at WFSB in Hartford, Connecticut. The News Director was Dick Ahles. He'd developed a solid newsroom with a talented team, and I wanted to work for him. After he looked at my demo reel he said, "I like your work, but we don't have an opening."

"I understand," I said. "Thanks very much for the interview."

Later that day, I called Ron Shapiro, who was one of my champions. Ron is a negotiations expert and top sports agent with clients in the Baseball Hall of Fame.

I said, "Ron, no luck at WFSB. They don't have an opening."

I figured Ron would say, "OK. Go back to the drawing board." Instead, he said, "OK. Go back to the News Director and tell him, 'I've watched your newscasts and I'm impressed with your team, and I don't want to miss the chance of working for you! What if I work half-time in the newsroom as a producer and half-time on the street as a reporter?'"

Over a few days, I practiced my pitch. Then, I called Dick Ahles back. He paused. "Hmm . . . Interesting . . . We've never done anything like that before. I'll let you know." Two weeks later, he called me back. "We figured it out. When can you start?"

The language that Ron gave me became an early Confidence Project Formula: Offer a Compliment and a Creative Solution, and then Practice to Build Confidence. Here's the million-dollar phrase: "*I don't want to miss the chance . . .*"

Ron's creative counsel has had a ripple effect. I've offered that million-dollar phrase to hundreds of people to use when applying for jobs or promotions, negotiating, or simply to connect with another person.

Here's how you can use it. "I don't want to miss the chance to . . ."

- share this article, podcast, TED Talk
- congratulate you
- thank you
- introduce you
- personally invite you
- let you know about
- recommend you
- work for you
- encourage you
- support you
- mentor you
- sponsor you

This phrase is compelling because you're telling people that they're special, and you *don't want to miss the chance* to remember them, honor them, thank them, support them, or work with them. And even though it may be something that you want (a job, recommendation, introduction, interview, a chance to mentor) it is also a way of making *other* people feel as if it's about *them*, too. And it is. The best opportunities are mutually rewarding.

Practice this million-dollar phrase. Pass it on to others. And along the way, look for opportunities to tell people, "I don't want to miss the chance."

The NOW Networking is alive and well in The World of Work today. "I don't want to miss the chance" of encouraging you to practice these skills to build your network and your career with ease and confidence.

CHAPTER 10

Confident Conversations

> *"Good conversation is as stimulating as black coffee, and just as hard to sleep after."*
> – Anne Morrow Lindbergh

"Tracy, I have good news and bad news." That's how one of my clients who's a senior manager started our phone call.

"OK. What's the good news?"

"The good news is I've been promoted."

"Fabulous! What's the bad news?"

"The bad news is, I'm an introvert. And I don't really like people, and now I'm in charge of 307 of them!"

We shared a good laugh!

Whether you see yourself as an introvert, extrovert, or somewhere in between, you can learn to be a good conversationalist and connect with your team, prospect, client, or a new friend. This is another example of the truism: Confidence can be learned.

Many people have worked remotely for a long time now, and for any number of companies, it may continue. No shoot-the-breeze watercooler conversations. No popping into people's offices to catch up. On video calls, we're hyper-focused on work topics. And when work teams have tried to be social, a friend wearily asked, "Does anybody really want another Zoom trivia night?" So here we are, heading back into the office occasionally or often. And we have to talk to each other. Are you wondering, "Remind me, how do I start a conversation again?!"

If you are self-conscious about your baseline conversation skills, or your conversation muscles have gotten flabby, you can practice the techniques in this chapter and tone up your dialogue muscles. You might even make them stronger than before. Strong is the new Confident!

The 10/5 way

This technique is a quick and easy way to connect. It's how companies like Walmart, Disney, and The Ritz-Carlton teach their employees to provide a better customer experience.

- If a staff member is within ten feet of a customer or guest, they're encouraged to look up and make eye contact.
- If a staff member is within five feet, they're asked to smile and say, "Hi."

A smile and a pleasant "Hello" go a long way.

The Art of Conversation
Six Techniques to Get a Conversation Started

No matter your industry or profession, you can start any conversation by practicing the golden rule of The Confidence Project: **Treat everyone as if they are the most important person in the room**. And they are. As you greet them, remember that everybody's favorite subject is themselves!

1. Give a Compliment

Everyone loves a compliment. Years ago, my dear friend, Miriam Thornburg who was 88 and elegant told me, "If you can't think of anything to say to someone, tell them, 'I like your shoes!'"

A longtime executive at HBO told me the opposite, "I never compliment my colleagues on their looks or what they are wearing. I compliment them on their effort or accomplishments: a creative idea, a solid presentation, a promotion, skillfully dealing with a difficult client, or meeting a demanding deadline."

Try these compliments:

- "We haven't met in person, but I heard your speech at the company all-hands, and it was terrific. I'm Gerry McNeal from the finance team."

- "Hi Julie. I read about your making the President's Circle (big award, new job, promotion, article you published, book you wrote, etc.) on LinkedIn. It's great to congratulate you in person. I'm Anna Arnell."

- Your presentation was spot on. And I appreciated you sharing that Nelson Mandela quote: "I never lose. I either win or learn." Exactly what we needed to hear.

You can also compliment people on the traits you admire about them. They are

- a great teammate
- a fierce competitor
- resilient
- compassionate
- respectful
- honest
- transparent
- accountable

- loyal
- flexible
- ethical
- generous

Every situation is unique. Use your judgment and access how well you know a person to determine the kind of compliment you give them. And it very well may be, "Cool glasses, nice jacket, or I like your shoes!"

Accept a Compliment with Confidence

When someone says, "You did a great job on that presentation," do you say, "Well, y'know, I got lucky. You all were a great audience."? Or, if you hear, "I admire your strategic thinking. You add a lot of value to our team," do you say, "To be honest, my thoughts are not as strategic as they seem. The team makes me look good."? Or, what about, "Those are great glasses!" Do you half smile and say, "Really? These things are ancient."?

When you brush off someone's compliment, it diminishes your success and perhaps their perception of you. They may think, "Maybe the presentation wasn't that good." It also dismisses the person who gave you the compliment, as if they have bad judgment and their opinion isn't valid.

On the surface, these responses sound modest or humble, but not confident. It's true that there's power in partnership and it's good to acknowledge the audience or team, but in that "I admire your strategic thinking" moment, the giver is praising *you*.

Here's how to accept a compliment with confidence. Start with, "Thank you."

- Thank you. I'm glad you enjoyed the presentation. It was a challenge to put it together, and you all were a great audience.

- Thank you for telling me. I'll remember that. I believe that strategy is critical to our success. And it's great to be part of the team.

- Thanks, I like my glasses, too!

Practice accepting and savoring accolades and then thank the giver with confidence.

---

2. Use Magic Words and Ask Kick Starter Questions

The best news reporters, hiring managers, and Oprah are skilled at asking open-ended questions. These questions get people talking. They often use The Magic Words: What? How? And tell me more. Let these Magic Words work for you. If you need ideas to chat with a new co-worker or someone you haven't seen since 2020, use Kick Starter Questions that begin with "What and How." These spark the conversation. "Tell me more" can help keep it going.

- What's it like to finally meet a co-worker in person who you've been working with for over two years?

- How are you encouraging your team to come back into the office?

- Tell me more about how you onboard people remotely.

See the complete list of Kick Starter Questions that use the Magic Words in the Appendix at the end of the book.

ESPN

My good friend Paul is an excellent athlete. He's into hiking, snowboarding, and mountain biking. But he's not into college or pro sports. The people he works with, though, are die-hard fans. So, here's his Cliff Notes way to connect. Every Sunday night, he watches fifteen minutes of ESPN highlights. On Monday morning, he's primed. "How about the Knicks' shot at the buzzer?" "What about the Ravens beating Detroit with Tucker's field goal? Sixty-six yards! That was crazy!" "What did you think about the spectacular finish at The Masters?" Guaranteed conversation Kick Starters!

3. Be Curious

CEOs tell us, they're looking to hire people with a high "CQ," a high Curiosity Quotient. How's your CQ? Here are ways to discover it.

- **Read:** Books, newspapers, magazines, publications with well researched content

- **Watch:** TED Talks, movies, documentaries, quality TV, and nature out your window or in your neighborhood

- **Listen:** Podcasts, lectures, webinars and conversations at meetings, networking events, industry conferences, or at a party

- **Pay Attention:** Tune in to people's body language, facial expressions, and tone of voice. This is an intuitive soft skill that's worth cultivating. Practice paying attention, and you'll be amazed at how people will tune in to you.

4. Research

Several years ago, my friend Joe virtually introduced Sheri Fitts and me. Sheri is a highly sought-after speaker and influencer in financial services marketing. Before we met in person, I read her LinkedIn profile and combed through her website. Tucked into the *Meet Sheri* page after the list of her offerings and accomplishments it says, "If all of that isn't enough to pique your interest, Sheri was also named Paper Girl of the Year (1976).[1] So, you can be confident that when you work with Sheri Fitts, she delivers." Research gold!

As we sat down for coffee, here was my conversation Kick Starter: "Hi Sheri. It's great to meet you. Congratulations on being named Paper Girl of the Year!" Boom! She burst out laughing. And the conversation flowed like a river!

The 5-Second Rule

"If you have an instinct to act on a goal, you must physically move within 5 seconds, or your brain will kill it."[2]

–Mel Robbins

Inspiration lasts one second. Talking yourself out of a good idea takes five. If you see someone at the office, at a conference, networking event, coffee shop, or in the lunchroom and you want to meet them, don't wait to feel ready, motivated, or confident. Use *The 5-Second Rule.* Count down, 5-4-3-2-1, and start walking towards them. Then, say, "Hi," introduce yourself, and ask a Kick Starter Question.

---

5. Make a Connection

Who do *you* know who *they* know?

- Ray Patel told me that you and I should meet because we both went to Michigan State. I'm Jim Bruce.

- Glenna White said that you're a runner and ran the Boston Marathon. Me too! What was your most memorable milepost?

- I was hoping to meet you today. Brett Klein said you might be at this conference. I'm Isabelle Geulin.

6. Listen

> *"I never learned anything while I was talking."*[3]
> – LARRY KING

Learning to listen takes practice. It's no different than practicing the guitar, chess, or tennis. To be an active listener:

- Pause. Quiet your own impulse to speak.

- Look the other person in the eye.

- Use nonverbals: smile, nod, lean in, and raise your eyebrows to show curiosity.

- Say the Magic Words: What? How? Tell me more.

Take the cell phone challenge.
How many times have you been in a meeting or dining with a group, and you hear the buzz? It's somebody's phone. The conversation stops. People get that sheepish look. "Is it mine?" Then they start fumbling. Searching pockets, purses, laptop cases, or among the collection of phones on the table. Next comes, "Sorry, I thought it was on silent." "Sorry, I need to take this call." "Sorry, I'll just be a minute." That's a buzz kill to a good conversation.

Next time, at a meeting or a meal, say this, "Everybody, let's be adventurous! I challenge us to turn off our phones and focus on each other. Let's put them on silent, face-down on the table, and the first person who checks their phone picks up the tab . . . or buys donuts for the next meeting!"

Note: If you think you'll have a heart attack with your phone on airplane mode, don't worry. You have your own Personal Assistant: **Voice mail!**

Smoothing Out Awkward Moments

Conversations take unexpected turns all the time. You can be having an interesting discussion, and then one comment can flip the conversation from curious to awkward or calm to confrontational. Trust your gut. If you don't feel comfortable with a divisive topic, or you're concerned about another person being offended, or the conversation veers into dangerous territory, try these statements:

- "There are various views on that issue, but I'd like to get back to what we were discussing."

- "That issue involves a different conversation. I'm happy to talk about it with you one-on-one at another time. Right now, let's hear more about Shola's proposal."

- "I want to be mindful of everyone in this group, and I don't think that discussing this topic serves all of us here. So, let's get back to the agenda."

- "I'm *not* comfortable talking about politics (religion, co-worker's personal life, salaries, masks, or vaccines) but I *am* interested in what you think about the speaker's ideas."

- "Milton, I know that issue is important to you. However, it doesn't affect everyone on the team. I'd be happy to talk about it after the meeting. Email me with some open times to follow up. Thanks."

Notice the "I Statements." They avoid judgment and lower the temperature. If you use a respectful tone, others in the group are likely to be relieved and may help steer the discussion towards a safer topic.

Note: If everyone else in the group seems comfortable with the conversation, but you're not, use one of the exit lines from Chapter 11, The NOW Goodbye, such as, "I'm going to step away now and let you all continue your conversation. See you later." Then, move on with confidence.

Taper and Follow Up

Occasionally, conversations become so entailed or expansive that you need to finish them at another time.

Several years ago, I was at a business lunch and excited to hear the keynote speaker. I was sitting next to a woman whose sister had passed away since the last time we'd seen each other. While we ate our lunch before the keynote took the stage, I said, "I am sorry to hear about your sister's passing. How are you doing these days?" That's all it took. The woman started at the beginning of her sister's diagnosis, recounting her many treatments. As she talked about the final days of her sister's life, I noticed the emcee approach the podium to introduce the speaker. My lunch partner kept talking. And talking. Of course. She'd lost her beloved sibling. I felt caught. In order to hear her story, listen to the keynote and not disturb others at our table, I needed to taper the conversation.

I leaned in, looked at her in the eye and quietly said, "I really want to finish hearing about your sister and how you're doing, so let's pick it up when the program is over." She heaved a huge sigh of relief. "OK. Good," she said. "I'd appreciate that. Thank you." Obviously, she was relieved not to rush through her story, knowing that she'd be able to keep talking about it after the event.

Here's another example of how to Taper and Follow Up. We've all been in the middle of a presentation or meeting when someone asks a thoughtful question or makes a comment that has little or nothing to do with the topic. Rather than letting the comment derail the meeting, Taper and Follow Up.

- "Josh, that's outside the scope of our meeting, so let's set aside time later to talk about it. Email me and we'll compare calendars."

- "That is an interesting thought. It may relate more to marketing rather than to this finance issue. Let's follow up after the meeting and set an appointment to talk about it."

- "Inga, that idea may take us in another direction. I need some time to think it through. Please send me an email to follow up."

Notice the consistent Confidence Project techniques: Using people's names, acknowledging, and "I Statements."

Three Sentences and a Period

If you think you over talk or over share, or someone has candidly told you, discipline yourself with Three Sentences and a Period. At the end of that third sentence, stop talking. Pause. Then ask something like,

- "What do you think?"
- "What's your advice?"
- "Tell me about your experience."

Then listen. When you offer this breathing space, it gives people a chance to catch up to what you've said, process it, and jump in if they want.

Don't create run-on sentences by sticking 'and' or 'uhh' between two thoughts. That will make your three sentences, more like six. You'll be rambling and people may space out. With those Fillers, you continue to claim the microphone or control the conversation. It's a monologue not a dialogue. It can be boring. And it can ding your reputation as someone who is tone-deaf or too self-involved.

Let Three Sentences and a Period be your go-to goal for a free-flowing conversation.

Being able to talk with each other is a glorious gift of being human. Trees communicate through their roots. Animals have their own secret languages. But as human beings, we get to hear others' voices. We discover each other's ideas, visions, concerns, and passions.

You can learn how to have Confident Conversations and be all the richer for it. Learn by listening. Watch others who do it well. The art of conversation is just that, art. Everyone has their own conversational style like different styles of music, dance, or poetry. The more we interact with each other, use "I Statements," are curious, make connections, and listen to understand, the deeper and more meaningful our relationships will be. And that builds confidence.

CHAPTER 11

The NOW Goodbye

Have you heard of the A.I. watch created at MIT? Its artificial intelligence tells you when you're boring! With voices only, it can detect happy, sad, or neutral tones. It measures your heartbeat, blood flow, and blood pressure. It calculates your energy, pitch, and vocabulary. With 83% accuracy, it detects if the person you are talking to finds you to be dull. And the watch buzzes you![1]

How many times have you been talking with someone and you think, "I cannot get out of this conversation. It's never going to end. I gotta go." When people drone on, often, all we hear is "blah blah blah."

The same thing now happens with video calls. In-person interactions have been quite limited during the pandemic, so many people still crave facetime and phone calls to relieve their isolation. While we all need to interact and communicate, it's possible to ignore important boundaries, like the person who can't stop talking once they have you cornered in a conversation.

It seems counterintuitive, but the reason to limit a conversation in terms of topic and time is to respect your work relationships and keep your clients. When conversations run too long, get off track, or become too personal, we hesitate to talk to that person the next time we see them. Or, if we receive their request for a virtual meeting or a phone call, it's tempting to say, "That won't work with my schedule." If *you're* the one who tends to talk too long, "leave 'em wanting more" by not dragging out conversations. This boundary is a solid strategy to strengthen your business bonds.

The building blocks of The NOW Goodbye are based on a four-part technique.

1. **Thank you**
2. **Acknowledgement**
3. **Farewell Phrase**
4. **Goodbye Gesture**

The following examples will show you how to mix & match and customize a NOW Goodbye based on your situation. Build, practice, and polish your Goodbyes and you will never wonder again, "How can I get out of this conversation?" or "I hope I haven't talked too long."

1. **Start with a Simple Thank You.**

    - Thanks for a great conversation. I really enjoyed it.
    - Thank you for your interest in my company.
    - Thank you for the opportunity to discuss our marketing plan.
    - Thank you for telling me what's going on with your business.
    - Thanks for our conversation today. I'll remember you.
    - Thank you for seeking me out. I'm glad we talked.
    - Thanks for listening to what's happening with me. I appreciate your interest.
    - Thank you for being generous with your advice.

2. **Add an Acknowledgement.** Acknowledging what the person has told you signals to them that you listened well and truly heard what they said. Here are some evergreen acknowledgements:

    - That was a fantastic/great/hilarious story.
    - I'm happy to hear what's been going on with you.
    - It's great to have an update on your business.
    - Good to hear your presentation/sales call/interview went well.

- I'm glad we could compare marketing strategies.
- It's been fascinating to hear about your program. I'd love to pick it up at another time to learn more.
- It's great that you had fun with your family/at your high school reunion/at the beach . . .
- Congratulations on your new client, job, project, promotion, puppy, baby, boat . . .
- I'm sorry to hear that this has been a hard time for you . . . (showing empathy)
- It sounds like you had a tough couple of years, but now things are getting better. I'm glad for you.

3. Add a Farewell Phrase. Remember to use their name to honor them.

- Parsa, I'm sure you want to get around to meet some other people here, so I'll let you go.
- Sophia Lyn, I want us both to have time to talk with other people today, so if I don't see you again before the convention is over, take care.
- Angelique, I hope you'll excuse me; I need to see Lisa before she leaves.
- Lauren, I have to switch gears. I have another meeting shortly. It was good to see you. Take care.

- Maurice, I have a call at the top of the hour (or in a few minutes), so I need to run. Bye or Bye for now.

- Dave, I saw you talking with Iteka Manzi. How do you know her?

  Note: I always ask how someone knows another person. Here's why. If the person you want to meet is a former bad boss or a difficult colleague, then the person you're asking for the introduction will probably not want to do that. Remember, they're talking with you now, not the other person.

- Here's the positive outcome.
  - Dave, I saw you talking with Iteka Manzi. How do you know her?
  - Oh, we worked together for 4 years. She's terrific!
  - Great, I've wanted to meet her. Will you introduce us, please?

- Would you share your contact information with me? I'd like to stay in touch.

- Do you have a business card? Thanks, I'll keep in touch.

- May I email you for a Virtual Coffee or lunch in the next few weeks?

- Let's connect on LinkedIn.

- I'm glad we had a chance to catch up. Before we say goodbye, I noticed on LinkedIn that you know Will Caplan. Would you be willing to make a virtual introduction?

- Best of luck with your new client, job, project.

- I hope you get that promotion. Keep me posted.

- Enjoy that new puppy, baby, boat . . .

- Have fun on your vacation!

4. Offer a Goodbye Gesture.

In general, the way you and the other person greeted each other will dictate your Goodbye Gesture. If you're both comfortable with handshakes, hugs, or high fives, then your Goodbye Gesture will probably be the same as your greeting. Relax and enjoy.

If you are *not* ready for a physical hello or goodbye, here are some comfortable contact-free Goodbye Gestures.

Keep these simple and choose the one that feels right for you. As always, make eye contact whether in person or on video calls. You want to close the conversation with a genuine connection and confidence. In person, a gracious, contact-free Goodbye Gesture is to tap your right palm over your heart. This way there's no awkwardness about whether to offer a handshake or hug. Other gestures include:

- Hands crossed over your chest
- A slight wave
- A nod of the head
- A brief bow
- A broad smile, your eye creases will show it's genuine

Graceful exit from an over-talker

If you're trying to end a conversation with someone who won't stop talking, say this:

You: "Frank, thanks for telling me about your fabulous vacation. I'm so glad you finally got away after two long years! I know we both have people we want to talk with, so I'll let you go."

Frank: "No, that's OK. I don't know anybody else here."

You: "OK. Well, you know what? I've wanted to meet Noni Smith-Ocho, and I see her over there. Let's both go over and introduce ourselves."

Success! You've made a graceful dismount from that conversation and are both kind and assertive by including this person in your next conversation, with confidence.

Here are Three Samples of an In-person NOW Goodbye

- Parsa, *thank you* for being generous with your advice tonight. And *congratulations* on your new baby. Be ready with new photos the next time we see each other! *I'm sure you want to get around* to meet some other people here, so I'll let you go. *Take care* and enjoy that baby!

- Jackie, *thank you* for sharing some details about what's going on with your business. *I'm sorry* it's been so hard. And *you've persevered!* Well done. Oh . . . *I'm noticing the time. I hope you'll excuse me*; I need to see Stacie before she leaves. *If we don't see each other again today*, take good care of yourself.

  Note: This is an appropriate use of "I'm sorry" to express empathy.

- Mary, *thanks* for a very interesting conversation. It was *good to hear* that your finalist presentation went well. *Before we say goodbye*, I noticed on LinkedIn that you know Will Caplan. Would you be willing to make a virtual introduction? Thank you . . . I'll message you with my contact information. Hope to see you again. *Bye for now.*

Choose your Goodbye Gesture and move on. Don't linger or you'll be right back to hearing "Blah Blah Blah!"

When you first start using this tool kit, choose one phrase from each category and mix and match to the situation: *Thank you. Acknowledgment. Farewell Phrase. Goodbye Gesture.* Like any confidence skill, take time to practice. Write down a few variations that sound like something you would comfortably say. Then rehearse. Record yourself on video, talk in the mirror to notice facial expressions and body language, or practice with a friend until you iron out the rough edges in your delivery.

The NOW Goodbye over the Phone

Caller ID is technology at its finest! If you recognize the caller and know they are a talker, set the expectations at the start and put a timeframe around the conversation. Then, you can bring the call to a close with clear boundaries. Notice the "I Statements" and the use of people's names to let them know they're important.

- Melissa, great timing! I have a meeting in 10 minutes, so I have 5 minutes for you! What can I do for you?

- Hi Brooke. Good to hear from you. I'm expecting a call in 10 minutes so I'm available for you for 5. How can I help you?

- Hi AJ. Your timing is impeccable! I was thinking about you a few days ago. I have another call in about 15 minutes, so let's take 10 minutes now to talk. What's on your mind?

- Hello Nia. Thanks for calling. Good to hear from you. A heads-up, please. I have about 30 minutes before my next meeting and one question for you. But you go first. Do you think we can finish up in 15 or 20 minutes?

To Wrap Up

- Noah, I promised we'd have a 30-minute call and we're almost there. May I answer one more question for you before we go? Or is there anything else I can do for you?

- Julian, my team is pinging me for my next meeting, so I have to say goodbye. It's been great talking with you. Take care.

- Ruben, we said we'd wrap up by noon and we're bumping up against the hour. So, lets sign off for now.

- Pennie, we're at time now, so I need to run. Thanks for the conversation. Hope to see you soon.

- Elizabeth, I'm glad we got to talk today. How would you like me to follow up?

One of my clients who's the president of a health care consulting firm found that his team regularly came to him with their issues, problems, and ideas. All those interruptions ate up hours in his work week. To take control of his time, I taught him how to master "I Statements" so that people feel heard and not offended. Here's what he says now:

- One of my goals this year is to be more conscious of my time and other people's, too. With that in mind, let's take 15 minutes to talk about this question now. If we need more time, we can reschedule.

- I've noticed that our 30-minute meetings often run long. This year, I'm committed to staying on time. So, from now on, I'll work to keep us on track.

- Let's stay on top of our time today. I have 10 minutes now. Let's jump in.

- That question deserves a 5-minute answer, but for the sake of this meeting's timeframe, here's my 1-minute response. We can talk about it in more detail at our staff meeting on Monday.

- That question deserves a 10-minute answer, and I don't have the time now. Please email my assistant to find 10 minutes on my calendar. I want to give you the time you need.

- I can tell that you're concerned about this matter (or excited about your idea), but I can't address it at the moment. Please talk with my assistant to find 20 minutes when I can give you my full attention.

Note: He shows empathy here *and* maintains his commitment to time management.

Consider this: Could this meeting be an email?

On video calls, tee up your Goodbye by defining the timeframe at the beginning of the call:

- I want to be mindful of everyone's time. We planned a 30-minute meeting, and I'll keep an eye on the clock.

- I have a hard stop at 2 p.m. Ben said he has a 3 o'clock. Let's stay on track, please.

- Ryan mentioned he has back-to-back meetings. Thanks for the heads up, Ryan. I'll keep track of the time for all of us.

- Everybody, I have another meeting right after this one, so I'd appreciate you all accommodating me by finishing up here by 2 p.m. How does that sound?

The timekeeper may want to put the 5-minute remaining alert in the chat.

However, if you say, "We only have 5 minutes left," then people will start looking at their phones and mentally checking out. Instead say:

- In the time we have left, let's circle the room for each of us to give a summary sentence. I'm happy to start. (Here's where you model a short wrap up.)

- In the interest of time, if you have additional suggestions, please them email to me.

- With an eye on our time, here's an executive summary. Does anyone want to add a final comment?

- Let's confirm the follow-ups or to-do list.

- When should we schedule our follow-up meeting? Next Tuesday, same time, works for me. How about everyone else?

These phrases keep people engaged through the closing minutes and lower their anxiety that the meeting will run late.

Say "Goodbye"

You may be thinking, "What do you mean, say goodbye? When a phone call is over, of course you say goodbye." These days, not necessarily. Back to the influence of popular culture. For some time, I've noticed that there are people of all ages, but mostly young professionals, who do not say "goodbye" on the phone. They simply hang up. Click.

It feels rude, as if the person is angry and hanging up on me. It's unintentional, of course. Perhaps it stems from texting where we rarely say "Goodbye." We simply stop texting. Regardless of why, be mindful that there is another human being on the other end of the telephone. Be courteous and say:

- Goodbye.
- Take care. Bye-Bye.
- Bye now.
- Bye for now.
- Talk with you later. Bye.

> *"Let's bring it in for a landing."*
> — JEFF WEBER

If you overtalk it's important to be honest with yourself and heed the nudge of my long-time friend, Jeff Weber. "Let's bring it in for a landing." You can begin to repair your reputation as an over-talker or any relationship damage you might have inadvertently caused by reverse engineering The NOW Goodbye. It's empowering to take the initiative and be known as the efficient colleague who respects others' time.

To establish better habits, set a time limit. As part of your greeting, state the amount of the time you would like for the conversation. If it is business related, have a note with bullet points for topics to cover—and stick to them. (Without notes, we wander.) Whether the call is planned or not, begin like this:

- "Hi Dan. It's Tracy Hooper. Thanks for taking my call. Is this a good time to talk?" *or* "Is this still a good time for us to talk?"
  - "Good. I've set aside 30 minutes to discuss the quarterly report. I won't keep you longer than that."
  - "I know it's late in the day, so let's jump right in."
  - "I want to honor our time, so I'll keep this brief, no more than 20 minutes. Does that work for you?"
  - "Great. I have a hard stop at 3, so I'll get right to the point."

Set the timer on your phone to alert you 5 minutes before the conversation is set to end. Wrap up the call by using The NOW Goodbye that is appropriate for the situation.

Begin the Goodbye with:

- I want to honor our time. I promised 20 minutes, and we're coming up on it.
- *Or* I want to be mindful of our time . . . We have 5 minutes left . . .

Then head right to . . .

Thank you:

- Thanks for our conversation today.
- Thanks for the opportunity to discuss . . .
- Thanks for the chance to review . . .
- Thanks for your insight into this situation.
- Thanks for your honest opinion or advice.

Acknowledgment:

- I'll remember the advice you offered.
- I respect your position on this situation.
- I am glad to hear what is going on with you.
- I appreciate your guidance/insight/perspective/feedback.

Farewell Phrase:

- I need to get to my next call. Take care.
- I promised our call would be 20 minutes, and we're close. So, let's finish up by looking at our calendars or by talking next steps.
- I said we'd be finished by 3, and we're bumping up to it.
- I'm glad we had a chance to catch up, Rob. Stay safe.

- My team is pinging me for my next meeting, so I'll say Goodbye. It's been great talking with you, Garrett. Stay well.

Contact-free Goodbye Gesture:

- Be sure to make eye contact and add a quick wave.

Here's a sample of a NOW Goodbye on the phone or video call.

> "Lindsey, *I want to honor our time.* I promised 20 minutes, and we're almost there. *Thanks* for your insight. I respect your position on this situation, and I'm glad we had a chance to talk about it. Now, *I'm getting pinged for my next meeting. So, I need to run. Bye for now.*"

For video, add a nod or wave and say, "*Thanks again and take care.*" Move on and leave 'em wanting more.

It doesn't matter whether you truly have a full schedule or a meeting at the top of the hour. The point is to be conscious of your tendency to drag out conversations and realize the importance of managing long and healthy relationships in The World of Work.

CHAPTER 12

The Hybrid Highway: Confidence Even in Uncertainty

> *"Be a Learner, not a Knower."*
> — Brené Brown

In the fall of 2021, a financial advising firm hired me for a professional development training. There was a team of twenty-five, half sitting in the newly renovated conference room and the other half on Zoom with their kitchen or living room in the background. I was on Zoom too, in my home office.

Each of the in-person folks could see their virtual teammates and me on the large, wall-mounted monitor. But those of us who were virtual couldn't see the entire team in the conference room because they were sitting 6 feet apart. The only people I could see clearly were the early birds who snagged seats close to the camera. Everyone in the conference room was wearing a mask, so their voices were muffled.

It didn't take long to see that the mix and match of in-person and remote was going to be tricky. The CEO was conflicted about where to look—at the people in the room or the team on the monitor. When he introduced me, he had moved out of the camera frame so I couldn't see or hear him anymore. Because I could only see about 25 percent of the people in the conference room, I was missing many micro-cues, and so was everyone else in the Zoom room. Q&A was a problem too; I couldn't hear the questions and kept asking, "Could you say that again, please?" It was clumsy and ate up time having to ask participants seated near the camera to repeat the questions for all of us.

So started our journey on The Hybrid Highway.

Collaboration equity
It doesn't matter where you and others are joining the meeting. In person or remote, everyone needs to be able

to see and hear each other. Google calls this Collaboration Equity, and it's an important part of the Hybrid Highway.

Technical Tips for Achieving Collaboration Equity:

- Install a camera(s) in the conference room so remote folks can see everyone in the actual room.

- Install a large monitor in your conference room. This way, everyone in the room can see the remote participants and any shared content.

- Make sure the whiteboard is visible to both in-person and remote attendees or use a common, digital document to share information and promote collaboration.

- If you are remote, lift your laptop to eye level so people feel as if you are looking at them across the table, not up at your ceiling.

- If one large monitor is not available, all the attendees in the conference room can dial into the meeting on their own laptop and keep themselves on mute.

- Set expectations at the top by acknowledging that it can be easier to recognize those in the room vs. those online. The message is: "No matter where you are, we want everyone's voice to be heard."

Welcome to the Hybrid Highway

Nobody's quite sure where their companies and workers are traveling along the Hybrid Highway, but in The World of Work now we all are on this bumpy road together. Business teams and leaders, individuals, and families are all trying to navigate the uncertain journey.

It's tough. Like someone who's trying to learn how to drive a stick shift and keeps stalling as they struggle to get into first gear, the world's businesses have sputtered, too. Nothing illustrates this predicament better than the continual shifts in the Return To Office plan: the Delta variant surged. Then Omicron forced companies and organizations to re-evaluate their return dates, again. Though many companies are going back, there are still degrees of uncertainty for RTO plans.

If you're exhausted, anxious, or short-tempered, there's good reason. Heidi Grant and Tal Goldhammer tell us why. "Our brains were not built for this much uncertainty."[1]

In their *Harvard Business Review* article, they explain that the human brain likes patterns. It also works most efficiently when we perform routine predictable tasks.[2] But when life becomes less controllable, we feel threatened, and our brains have a hard time with the "unknowns." The feeling of uncertainty registers as danger. Continually feeling threatened or scared "leads to decreases in motivation, focus, agility, cooperative behavior, self-control, sense of purpose and meaning, and overall well-being."[3] With the pandemic still hovering, remote work, and the ever-changing RTO plans, along with other global concerns, we all have reason to feel exhausted, anxious, and short-tempered.

Find Your Lane on the Hybrid Highway

Every work situation is on the table right now—from remote-first, to hybrid schedules, to full-time RTO. Surveys show that most employees want a hybrid schedule.[4]

Jessica is ready to move from fully remote to a hybrid schedule. As the VP of Communications for an association representing hundreds of companies across the U.S., she told me that one WFH challenge was the lack of personal, casual interaction with her colleagues. "It's that cultural piece that if you're never together in person, it can chip away at your connections and natural conversations, which are the building blocks of trust." Flexibility is the million-dollar word. In fact, research also says that what many people really want is autonomy, the ability to choose whatever hybrid, remote, or full-time schedule works best for them.[5] Jessica says her perfect scenario would be WFH 3 days with 2 days at headquarters. That's when she hopes she and her team will have time for natural interactions, conversations, and collaboration. And she's looking forward to those civilized "collisions" where she and the rest of her colleagues will "collide" in the hallway, around the water cooler and in the lunchroom.

After all this time physically away from each other, psychologists say people need opportunities to really catch up about their lives, reconnect, debrief, decompress, and delight in each other. We need to spark connections to bring back that sense of belonging and a common purpose.

> *"I love being back in the office a few days a week. Now I don't have to schedule a 15-minute Zoom for a 2-minute conversation."*
> – MATT, MINNEAPOLIS, MN

Tom has had a great engineering career. For almost thirty years, he's been with a Fortune 50 tech company with a sprawling campus. Before COVID, Tom traveled to Europe from the west coast every two weeks. The shutdown ended those in-person meetings with his clients and team. Tom says, "Every Tuesday since March 2020, I have a meeting at 3:30 a.m. It's either that, or I sit on a plane for fourteen hours every fourteen days. The early morning meetings are a small sacrifice for the taste of freedom."

For millions, the pandemic has presented the possibility that work does not have to be the be-all-end-all. It's a dance and involves compromise. What you want, what the company or organization wants from you, and how you determine the best fit for your life may be influenced by where you are in your career and your future goals.

The Barbell Effect

Harry Klaff introduced me to the concept of the Barbell Effect.[6] Harry is President of Clients at Avison Young, a global commercial real estate company.[7] As Harry describes it, "The barbell has younger workers at one end and older workers at the other. In general, many leaders say that younger and older employees want to come back to the office. The workers in the middle, in mid-career, often with families, want more flexibility."

For practical reasons, young professionals may prefer the office because their Wi-Fi at home is unreliable, or their background is unprofessional, or they're living with roommates who are Zooming non-stop, too. For professional growth, young people find that the workplace is where they can listen and learn, make friends, find mentors, and literally be seen. They have opportunities to rub elbows with senior management and might be top of mind for an invitation to join meetings because they are physically present. Junior staff learn, when they invest in relationships with seasoned pros, that those influential leaders can advocate for a stretch job or promotion for them. These experiences build confidence. Included at this end of the barbell with young employees are those who prefer to be in the office because they like the structure, setting, camaraderie, and the focus that working in a business space can provide.

> *"I'm psyched to see people again. It feels like I've been living inside a video game."*
> – Raul, Atlanta, GA

What about the other end of the barbell? Harry told me that older employees may prefer to be in the office to stay relevant, be part of the mainstream, and mentor those younger people. By sharing their wisdom, experience, and success strategies, they can influence new, eager professionals, help onboard and integrate new team members, and continue to impact the bottom line. That experience reinforces their confidence, too.

Those workers in the middle of the barbell are generally between their 30s and 50s. They are considered by corporate America as the future of business. They're at the top of their careers, and in today's tight labor market, they have an outsized say in how they want to work. For this group, flexibility is essential. These prized employees are emerging leaders who have the added responsibilities of families and other commitments, and they want the flexibility for it all—especially working mothers.

During the pandemic, many moved from their cramped apartments in big cities with long commutes to smaller towns with a slower pace and a bigger house. Twenty steps from their kitchen to their home office is now an expectation and with the strong demand for talent, it's not going away. If the labor market softens, these employees may not have as much leverage as they do now. Until then, however, those in the middle of the barbell can seemingly call the shots about their schedules and enjoy what they feel is a better quality of life.

Determining . . . and Getting . . . What you Want

Knowing what you need from a hybrid work arrangement clarifies your goals and helps you prepare to make your case to your boss. Ask yourself, "What days do I want and need to work from home, and when is it better for me to be in the office?" Be honest with yourself about what makes you productive and contributes to your well-being. Keep in mind your priorities for life outside of work. Whatever solution works for you must also support your co-workers and drive performance in your department. Consider how your preferred work arrangement will impact your career growth, your team members, and your manager.

The Confident Ask

Knowing what to ask for and how to ask for it are critical. After you've identified what you want in your schedule, here are guidelines for your Confident Ask.

Time it Right

- It may work to propose your hybrid schedule during a performance review or one-on-one meeting.

- Don't spring the conversation on your boss casually. Instead, schedule a specific time to meet.

- Send an email to make your request.

- Make the topic of the meeting clear. "I'd like 30 minutes with you to talk about my schedule, please."

- Honor your promise of the 30-minute meeting.

Make Your Ask Specific and Convincing

- Be realistic. Remember your proposal has to work for the whole company, not only you. Pick the points you care about most.

- Ask your peers what they most need from you and how your days away from the office will affect them and highlight how you have incorporated those needs into your plan.[8]

- Which days do you want to work from home and why?

- How will this schedule improve your productivity? Give specific examples of how WFH during the pandemic improved your results.[9]

- What is your enhanced communication plan for trust building and staying in sync with your supervisor and your team?

- Consider being in the office for weekly team meetings, collaboration sessions, and trainings. If you know the end of the quarter or beginning of the fiscal year are exceptionally busy, tell your manager that you are willing and available to be in-office full time at those times.

- How will your results be measured for your out-of-office days?

- Demonstrate that you have a professional home office setting with good Wi-Fi, lighting, clutter-free or virtual background, etc.[10]

Emphasize Benefits and Accountability

- "I'll be able to work more efficiently from home and provide faster turnaround times since I can work without distractions."

- "Here's an example that highlights my flexibility in responding to an unexpected issue, after hours."[11]

- Give concrete examples of team synergy, greater creativity or efficiency, and close work relationships during the months of WFH. "We've used Slack and Google docs to stay aligned, and, for example, we finished the HighTower proposal before the deadline."[12]

- Assuming you want to stay at the company, include how hybrid work has increased your job satisfaction and your performance.[13]

- Your manager is likely receiving requests from other team members who have their own work schedule priorities so suggest a trial period. "I understand this is a demanding time for you. I'd like to suggest a reasonable time frame for us to test out my schedule. Perhaps 1-3 months. Then we can re-evaluate. What are your thoughts?" or, "Would you like a few days to think about it?"

- There is a lot to discuss in 30 minutes. Your boss has to know how your schedule will benefit them. Be ready to compromise.

Measurable Results

- Agree on results that can be tracked and verified during the trial. Keep detailed records of the work you complete. "Here's one way for me to measure my effectiveness."

- Communicate more than usual. Consider regular check-ins.

- Take on a stretch assignment during your trial, offer to help others on your team, and complete work ahead of a deadline to increase the chances of getting your schedule extended.

- Schedule a meeting for the end of the trial period. Have a candid discussion about what worked well, what didn't, and what adjustments need to be made to make the hybrid schedule work for everyone involved.

Express Sincere Gratitude

- Close your meeting with, "Thank you for the opportunity to talk about both of our expectations of my schedule. I appreciate your challenges to manage the team, our work product, and answer to the broader demands of the company."

- If your manager seems resistant to your plan, stay professional and be mature. Make sure your words and body language align.

- Even if you don't get the result you hope for, you will have set the stage for the next time you ask.

Practice, Practice, Practice

- Roleplay in front of a friend until you can run through your talking points smoothly.

- Practice Q&A. Let your practice partner ask questions and interrupt you as in real life. You'll feel less rattled if this happens during your meeting.

- Practice using "I Statements." For example, "I find that I am more productive . . .I prefer . . .I feel confident communicating remotely. I'll be available to . . ."

- Know your points well but have your notes with you. "I've brought my notes to stay on track."

Hybrid Is the NOW Benefit

At a non-profit organization in Northern Virginia, hybrid work is so successful that it's been added to the employee benefits package. "The feedback is fabulous," says the SVP of Human Resources. "Morale is high and so is productivity. I save my project-focused work for my at-home days because I have fewer distractions."

Responsive Leadership

If you're a leader, The World of Work today is highly challenging. You have to pivot again and again, regulate your own emotions about the challenges, and guide your team along on the Hybrid Highway. To help them adjust to the RTO and learn what their concerns are, ask questions and stay in touch. Here's what the experts suggest:

- Send out regular anonymous surveys to gauge how your team is faring and feeling

- Hold regular 1:1 check-ins without an agenda

- Encourage people to express themselves by acknowledging them, validating what they say, and offering open-ended questions such as *What? How?* and *Tell me more.*

  - "What is the biggest adjustment you're dealing with right now?
  - "I can see why this is exhausting for you."

- "How can I best support you right now?"
- "How are you feeling about being back in the office? *or*
- "How are you feeling about working from home while others have returned to the office?
- What would be helpful for you right now?"

Instead of asking someone on your team, "How are you doing?" ask them, "How are you doing today?" The word today will help them focus on the present moment and not give you a play-by-play of their life since the pandemic started. You may then offer:

- "I hear you when you say returning to the office *or* your new work schedule has been hard on you."
- "Tell me more about that."
- "Would it help to hear some advice I got recently that's supported my adjustment in returning to the office *or* to a new work schedule?"

These questions will help people sort through their feelings, pinpoint what they need, and inform what you can do to support them, if possible. As a leader, you're not responsible for being the fixer, but you can help your teammates feel safe to share what's going on with them and supported to do their best work. Finally, remember to say, "Thank you for filling me in. I know it can feel vulnerable. I appreciate your honesty and trust in me."

Listening isn't agreeing.

Active listening is truly hearing and empathizing with another person. Whether you're on the team or a team manager, take time to listen to your colleague. This is especially important when you're negotiating or disagreeing. Listening opens the door to trust, collaboration, and solutions.

Here's how to actively listen

- Make eye contact. Paraphrase what you have heard. "What I hear you saying is . . ."

- Lean in. Nod. Empathize. "I can appreciate how hard this is for you . . ."

- Be curious. "Say more." or "Tell me more about that . . ." or "Keep going . . . "

- Mirror or repeat back what you've heard. "It sounds like what you're concerned about is . . ."

Your Mindset: Fixed or Growth

For leaders and team members alike, your mindset may be the greatest factor in determining how you adapt and thrive in The World of Work today. Dr. Carol Dweck is a Stanford

Psychologist who coined the terms "fixed mindset" and "growth mindset." People with a fixed mindset believe that their talents and intelligence are fixed; they can't be enhanced or developed. They also believe that their talent alone will give them an easy path to success.

"In a growth mindset," Dr. Dweck writes, "people believe that their most basic abilities can be developed through dedication and hard work—brains and talent are just the starting point. This view creates a love of learning and a resilience that is essential for great accomplishment."[14]

In The World of Work today, curiosity and resilience are key confidence skills. With a revolution going on in the workplace, opt for growth. Prove that you're willing to embrace challenges, persist during tough times, and learn from criticism and failure.[15] These are the traits that confident people bring to work every day, no matter where their office might be located.

Here are three practices that will promote a growth mindset and ease the journey along the Hybrid Highway.

1. Shift from trial & error to trial & learning.

The old "Trial & Error" mindset is all about success or failure. Right or wrong. Good or bad. When you shift to "Trial and Learning," you give yourself permission to focus on your progress, not perfection. And this mindset gives you the time to make mistakes, regroup, and keep going.

2. Establish after-action review.

Bobby Herrera is a former military man. He has a deep understanding of "debrief" training to learn and improve on new projects and initiatives. Now the CEO of Populus Group, Herrera uses "after-action reviews" where his entire team meets and talks openly about "what happened, why, and how to improve."[16] No finger-pointing, griping, or blaming allowed. Together, they develop strategies for future successes.

3. Seek advice from people who don't think like you and be willing to change your mind.

According to Career Coach Michael Thompson, confident people actively seek advice from people who hold a variety of viewpoints.[17] A diversity of opinions helps avoid group think and the echo chamber effect. Confident people are willing to broaden their perspective and accept new ideas to help them move forward.[18]

Personal Board of Advisors

If you're a leader, you'll be a better one if you take care of yourself.

Recruit a Personal Board of Advisors. This is a small group of selected individuals who you can lean on for support and advice. Consider a trusted colleague, a leader who you admire inside or outside of your organization, a mentor, or a sponsor. You can even ask a long-time friend who knows you well, wants the best for you, and with whom you can be vulnerable, honest, and completely yourself.

Schedule a regular time to meet one-on-one, such as monthly, quarterly, semiannually, or as needed. These are 911 calls! Then, invite the entire Board to gather annually either virtually or in person. This is a chance for the Board to meet each other. It's also an opportunity for you to acknowledge each person's specific ideas and insights and thank the group for their contributions and guidance.

The pandemic has changed all of us in some way. Don't lead alone. Your team and your well-being deserve the benefit you'll receive from your Personal Board of Advisors.

The Great Resignation or A Great Reshuffling

Perhaps you've made The Confident Ask and didn't get the result you wanted. Or, you have a good manager who tried to accommodate your requests but couldn't make it happen. Or, you have re-evaluated the work you're doing and don't want to deal with the stress and strain of your company or industry anymore. Or, your priorities have changed and no matter what accommodations your boss has made, or how well stocked the office bar is with free beer and bourbon or Pringles and pool tables, you have decided to take the off-ramp along the Hybrid Highway and join the Great Resignation.[19]

If any of these scenarios describes your situation, now may be a great time to look for a job because employers are looking for you! Job openings have been near a record high,[20] so it may be worthwhile to consider changing industries, or your career path, or your personal direction. What are your interests? What have you always wanted to do? Follow your curiosities. Keep a journal. Use your phone to record voice memos for yourself. Give your notes folder on your phone an optimistic name and keep adding ideas there. Talk with others who have made changes and are happy about it. Ask those Kick Starter Questions, then listen.

If you're ready, you might become part of a Great Reshuffling. That's what labor economist, Arindrajit Dube calls those workers who leave bad jobs for better ones or entrepreneurs who've decided to start their own businesses.[21] Whatever you decide, know that you can leverage the skills and techniques in The NOW Hello to do the work you are equipped and eager to do.

Leave a Clean Campsite

In the great outdoors, a responsible camper always leaves a clean camp site: trash picked up, campfire doused, coals removed, and all belongings packed up and taken with you. It's equally important to "leave a clean campsite" when you're leaving a job whether voluntarily or involuntarily.

Clean up your workspace and any relationships that were difficult or may have gone sideways. The world is small. The internet is vast. And many industries are tightknit. Who knows? Your current colleague may become a future colleague or even your future client. Don't be a flame thrower as you leave the organization. Remember, you take yourself and your reputation wherever you go. Leave with dignity and a good reputation. Your future self will thank you.

Confidence Accommodates Change

No matter where you're traveling along the Hybrid Highway, now is the time to leverage new confidence skills for The World of Work. Use the strategies in this chapter to get the work arrangements that are right for you and for your company or to find a new position or career path. Add additional strategies to help you manage uncertainty, expand your perspective, and build your confidence.

Think of the Hybrid Highway as an opportunity instead of a problem. After so much has happened in the world, it's clear that we are no longer figuring out how we get back to normal, but how we get back to life.

CONCLUSION

Betty Lee and Bob Sweeney were two of my parents' best friends. At a party celebrating their 25th wedding anniversary, Bob read Betty Lee a card that said, "Betty Lee, thank you for 20 of the best years of my life." My mother looked at him with surprise. "Bob, you two have been married for 25 years." Bob grinned. "Well, you know, some years are better than others!"

Yes, some years are better than others.

Indeed, the past few years have been ones that many people would rather forget. They have challenged, shaken, and upended every part of our lives. At the same time, there are issues that have been amplified since 2020 that we must *not* forget: health disparities, the climate crisis, systemic racism, and global conflicts, to name a few. For sure, we are experiencing non-stop, back-to-back moments of challenge and change.

Still, I believe that confidence accommodates challenge and change. Being confident doesn't mean that you're never afraid or intimidated. It means that you have practiced certain skills so that even in the midst of change, you know what to say or do next. This knowing lowers your anxiety and allows you to focus on your job and the relationships you want to build and nurture.

If turbulent years have shown us anything, it's that we need each other and we want to be together. We crave connection. We yearn to belong. And we can achieve all of these aspirations when we communicate clearly. Good communication is our personal currency. It attracts us to each other. It helps build trust. It leads to civilized conversations and helps us to get along better.

If you embrace the mindset and skillset inside The NOW Hello, it will enhance your leadership. It will help define you as a solid team member. It will boost the reputation of your organization and enhance your own reputation, as well.

If you practice the techniques for positive posture and presence in person and online, it will help further your career.

If you champion genuine connection through vibrant, rich, curious conversations, it will deepen relationships in every part of your life.

If you elevate your language, people will listen to you more. They will also see you as eloquent, calm, dignified, poised, optimistic, authentic, self-assured and a person they can believe in. In short, you will have more confidence in yourself, and others will have more confidence in YOU!

It's a spiral upward!

Give yourself permission to change. Take pleasure in progress. The shift in your confidence will transform you inside and out and carry you forward personally and professionally in The World of Work.

Thank you for reading *The NOW Hello*.

APPENDIX

Magic Words and Kick Starter Questions

> *"In 35 years as a hair stylist, I've gotten 10 college degrees from all the conversations I've had with my clients. It starts by being curious."*
> – ROB DEBNAM

When you begin a question with What or How, it communicates your curiosity and shows others that you are interested in their thoughts, ideas, feelings, opinions, and stories. It gives people a chance to express their creativity, engages their imagination, and offers them the opportunity to problem solve out loud. Most importantly, voicing these Magic Words and adding Tell me more, invites a richer conversation and can start to build, or re-build, a relationship.

Work

What do you like best about your job?

What's the most interesting part of your work?

What's your biggest professional challenge?

What motivated you to leave your company?

What are you interested in doing next?

How do you recommend I approach this project?

How did you deal with . . .?

How did you come up with that idea?

How would you describe your ideal client/co-worker/boss?

Work Life and Company Culture
Home

What is/was the biggest perk of working from home?

What inspires you when you work from home?

What is your most important work boundary at home?

What's the biggest challenge of working from home?

How do you find a rhythm when you work from home?

Office

What's been the biggest adjustment to being back in the office?

APPENDIX – Magic Words and Kick Starter Questions

What is your most important boundary at the office?

How are you reconnecting with people?

Hybrid

What does your hybrid schedule look like?

What's your biggest adjustment now that people are coming back to the office?

How's it going for you?

Team

What excites you most about the changes our team is making?

What are you doing to manage the stress we feel on our team right now?

How have you stayed motivated?

What inspires you most about the leadership in your company?

What are the values of your company culture? What are your personal values? Do they align?

How is your company building culture?

How are you adjusting to a new job that began virtually and now is fully in person or hybrid?

How do you stay in front of senior management when you're remote?

Leadership

What was your first job and what did you learn from it?

What do you think is the biggest misconception about good leadership?

What is your leadership philosophy?

What character traits do you look for when you hire?

What's it like to create a company culture for new hires?

How has your leadership style changed since COVID?

How do/did you manage your team remotely?

How do/did you onboard people remotely?

How do/did you create a company culture for new hires when they are remote?

How do/did you deal with . . .?

How do you take care of your own well-being while continuing to care for a company or your team?

How do you manage your stress?

Arts and Culture

What books are on your bedside table?

What movies are your recommending these days?

What movie do you watch when you need a pick-me-up?

What are you binge-watching lately?

What's your favorite app?

What's your favorite podcast?

What's your new favorite podcast?

What songs are on your favorite playlist?

What's the one song you can listen to over and over?

What's your favorite kind of live event?

Pets!

Everyone has a pet or knows someone who does.

I hear you have a dog now. Tell me all about them!

Personal Reflections and Values

What gets you out of bed in the morning?

What is the best compliment you can give to someone else?

What is an inspirational quote that you try to live by?

What are you curious about?

What are you passionate about?

What are your best self-care practices to avoid burnout?

What breaks your heart? (This shows what people care about.)

What is the kindest gesture someone has done for you? Or, done for you lately?

What kind gesture are you doing for others these days?

What are you most grateful for?

Introspection

What's your superpower?

What's your take on . . .?

What are your thoughts about . . .?

What are you afraid of?

What are you optimistic about?

What keeps you hopeful?

What do you think is the difference between optimism and hope?

What daily ritual(s) keep you moving forward?

What do you try to pay attention to every day?

What's at the top of your to-do list every morning?

What is the one personal goal you'd like to accomplish this year?

What do you read first in the morning?

What did you used to believe that you couldn't do . . . that you can do now?

What course do you wish you had taken in school that would have benefited you as an adult?

APPENDIX – Magic Words and Kick Starter Questions

What subject in school did you not take seriously that in retrospect you wish you had?

What is the mantra that makes you feel confident/calm/inspired/content during a stressful day?

What do you do to stay motivated?

What are you most proud of in your life? Career?

What are the lessons you learned in COVID times? (work, personal, physical, emotional, spiritual, etc.)

What do you want people to know about you at your 10th, 25th, 50th reunion?

What do you look for in a friend?

What do you know for sure?

What do you want to be remembered for?

FUN!

What do you do for fun?

What are your hobbies?

What does a social life look like for you post COVID?

How has your idea of fun changed since COVID?

What's your idea of a great vacation?

What's the perfect day off look like to you?

Who would you most like to have dinner with . . . living or passed? (Not a "what" or "how" question, but it's a great Kick Starter with the follow up: Why? Tell me more!)

Life Lessons:

What's your biggest takeaway from living through a pandemic, so far?

What event or experience made you realize you were in over your head?

What did you do about it?

What did you learn during a tough time that made you wiser, more careful, or more carefree?

What lessons will you carry forward from . . . ?

What is the lesson that's taken you the longest to learn?

What is one belief you used to have that you don't believe anymore?

What is important to you now?

What quality do you admire most in others?

What would you say to your younger self about how you can grow genuine confidence and how long it can take?

What (still) inspires you?

What is the best compliment you can give?

What is the best feedback you have been given? Did you act on it?

How do you most appreciate getting feedback?

How do you create ease in your life?

How have you changed since 2020?

Offer help or empathy

What do you need me to know?

How can I be of service or help you?

Ask for a Story

What's your worst experience that made your best story?

What's the best trip you ever took?

What did your grandparents try to teach you that you didn't pay attention to as a child?

What do you wish you'd asked your grandparents?

What is the luckiest thing that's ever happened to you?

How did you get interested in the law, medicine, architecture, gardening, bird watching, running, music, writing, traveling?

How did you get started in real estate, high tech, teaching?

Tell me about you.

Tell me more. Keep going. It's such a good story!

ENDNOTES

Chapter 1 Mindset + Skillset

1. Microsoft, "The Next Great Disruption Is Hybrid Work—Are We Ready?" March 22, 2021, https://www.microsoft.com/en-us/worklab/work-trend-index/hybrid-work.

2. Microsoft, "The Next Great Disruption."

3. Stephanie Vozza, "How the 'Zoom Ceiling' Might Hurt Your Chance of Promotion," Fast Company, January 26, 2022, https://www.fastcompany.com/90715455/how-the-zoom-ceiling-might-hurt-your-chance-of-promotion#:~:text=%E2%80%9CRemote%20workers%20aren't%20getting,less%20likely%20to%20get%20promoted-.%E2%80%9D.

4. Microsoft, "The Next Great Disruption."

5. Felix Richter, "The Great Resignation Record: How Many Americans Left Their Jobs in November 2021?" World Economic Forum, January 18, 2022, https://www.weforum.org/agenda/2022/01/the-great-resignation-in-numbers-record/.

6. Arindrajit Dube (@arindube), "The Great Reshuffling continues, as workers leave bad jobs for better ones…," Twitter, March 9, 2022, https://twitter.com/arindube/status/1501605259117928451

7. Alexander Samuel and Tara Robertson, "Don't Let Hybrid Work Set Back Your DEI Efforts," *Harvard Business Review*, October 13, 2021, https://hbr.org/2021/10/dont-let-hybrid-work-set-back-your-dei-efforts.

8. Emilie Le Beau Lucchesi, "The Stresses of the Way We Work Now," *New York Times*, May 14, 2020, https://www.nytimes.com/2020/05/14/well/mind/coronavirus-work-stress-unemployment-depression-anxiety.html.

9. Emma Goldberg, "Say Hello Again to the Office, Fingers Crossed," *New York Times*, February 24, 2022, https://www.nytimes.com/2022/02/24/business/return-to-work-office.htm.

10. Tom Randall et al., "More Than 10.8 Billion Shots Given: COVID-19 Tracker," *Bloomberg*, updated March 4, 2022, https://www.bloomberg.com/graphics/covid-vaccine-tracker-global-distribution/.

11. Naomi Kresge and Tim Loh, "From Pandemic to Endemic: Can 2022 Succeed Where 2021 Failed?" *Bloomberg*, January 15, 2022, https://www.bloomberg.com/news/articles/2022-01-15/from-pandemic-to-endemic-can-2022-succeed-where-2021-failed.

12. The concept of psychological safety was defined by organizational behavioral psychologist Amy Edmondson. Amy Edmondson, "Psychological Safety and Learning Behavior in Work Teams," *Administrative Science Quarterly* 44, no. 2 (1999): 350–83, https://doi.org/10.2307/2666999.

Chapter 2 Plan + Practice = The NEW Hello

1. Romy Ellenbogen, "As People Go Back out in Public, Experts Weigh in on Where the Risks Are," *Tampa Bay Times*, May 27, 2020, https://www.tampabay.com/news/health/2020/05/27/as-people-go-back-out-in-public-experts-weigh-in-on-where-the-risks-are/.

Chapter 3 Impress + Influence

1. Eric Wargo, "How Many Seconds to a First Impression?," APS Observer 19, no. 7 (July 1, 2006), https://www.

psychologicalscience.org/observer/how-many-seconds-to-a-first-impression.

2. "Micro Expressions|Facial Expressions," Paul Ekman Group, accessed November 9, 2020, https://www.paulekman.com/resources/micro-expressions/.

3. Avital Andrews, "Your Brain Decides Whether to Trust Someone in Milliseconds," *Pacific Standard,* August 29, 2014, https://psmag.com/social-justice/trust-brain-decides-milliseconds-89771.

4. Susan Pinker, "The Science of Staying Connected," *Wall Street Journal,* April 2, 2020, https://www.wsj.com/articles/the-science-of-staying-connected-11585835999.

5. Pinker, "The Science of Staying Connected."

6. Jen Murphy, "How to Smize (Smile With Your Eyes) When You're Wearing a Mask," *Wall Street Journal,* August 26, 2020, https://www.wsj.com/articles/smize-mask-coronavirus-pandemic-covid-tyra-banks-reopen-restaurants-11598463705.

7. Murphy, "How to Smize."

8. Terry Gross, "Seth Meyers' 'Late Night' Challenge: What To Do With His Hands," *Fresh Air,* Recorded 2014, accessed November 10, 2020, https://www.npr.org/2014/04/23/306155626/seth-meyers-late-night-challenge-what-to-do-with-his-hands.

9. Susan Weinschenk, "Your Hand Gestures Are Speaking For You," *Psychology Today,* September 26, 2012, http://www.psychologytoday.com/blog/brain-wise/201209/your-hand-gestures-are-speaking-you.

10. Weinschenk, "Your Hand Gestures."

11. Joel Stein, "The Video Call Is Starting. Time to Put on Your Zoom Shirt," *New York Times,* June 29, 2020, https://www.nytimes.com/2020/06/29/business/zoom-shirt.html.

12. Emily VanSonnenberg, "Enclothed Cognition: Put On Your Power!" *Positive Psychology News* (blog), May 21, 2012, https://positivepsychologynews.com/news/emily-vansonnenberg/2012052122126.

13. Louise Bernardi, "The Power of Cognitve Clothing," accessed March 5, 2022, http://louise.net.au/2021/08/12/the-power-of-cognitive-clothing/.
14. Jacob Gallagher, "Why Some Men Are Still Wearing Suits to Work from Home," *Wall Street Journal*, January 21, 2021, https://www.wsj.com/articles/meet-the-men-wearing-suits-to-work-from-home-11611249573.
15. Anne Marie Chaker, "What to Wear Now? The Pandemic Closet Surge Is Under Way," *Wall Street Journal*, December 1, 2021, https://www.wsj.com/articles/what-to-wear-closet-purge-donate-clothes-fashion-pandemic-sweatpants-11638372595.
16. Katharine K. Zarrella, "Zoom Shirts Are Out. Zoom Fashion Is In," *Wall Street Journal*, February 19, 2021, https://www.wsj.com/articles/zoom-shirts-are-out-zoom-fashion-is-in-11613762374.
17. Zarrella, "Zoom Shirts Are Out."
18. Jamie Waters, "What Does Men's Business Casual Look Like Now?" *Wall Street Journal*, February 8, 2022, https://www.wsj.com/articles/business-casual-mens-hybrid-work-dress-code-11644274239

Chapter 4 Presence + Posture + Power

1. Michelle Graff-Radford, "Sitting Is the New Smoking," Mayo Clinic, February 11, 2020, https://connect.mayoclinic.org/blog/living-with-mild-cognitive-impairment-mci/newsfeed-post/sitting-is-the-new-smoking/.
2. Olga Khazan, "How Texting Hurts Your Neck," *The Atlantic*, November 18, 2014, https://www.theatlantic.com/health/archive/2014/11/what-texting-does-to-the-spine/382890/.
3. Khazan, "How Texting Hurts Your Neck."
4. Amy Cuddy, "Your Body Language May Shape Who You Are," filmed June 2012 in Edinburgh Scotland, TedGlobal video, 20:46, https://www.ted.com/talks/amy_cuddy_your_body_language_may_shape_who_you_are.

5. Cuddy, "Your Body Language."
6. Jessica L. Tracy and David Matsumoto, "The Spontaneous Expression of Pride and Shame: Evidence for Biologically Innate Nonverbal Displays," *Proceedings of the National Academy of Sciences of the United States of America* 105, no. 33 (August 19, 2008): 11655–60, https://doi.org/10.1073/pnas.0802686105.
7. Cuddy, "Your Body Language."
8. Linda Brice, personal communication, for more information on Linda Brice and the importance of voice see the website *Transformation Voice* at https://www.transformationalvoice.com/.

Chapter 5 Camera Confidence + Connection

1. Travis Bradberry, "Multitasking Damages Your Brain and Your Career, New Studies Suggest," *TalentSmart* (blog), accessed November 10, 2020, https://www.talentsmart.com//articles/Multitasking-Damages-Your-Brain-and-Your-Career,-New-Studies-Suggest-2102500909-p-1.html.
2. Bradberry, "Multitasking Damages Your Brain."
3. Patience Haggin, "Next in Videoconferencing—Hiding Your On-Screen Double Chin," *Wall Street Journal*, May 21, 2020, https://www.wsj.com/articles/coronavirus-videoconferencing-hiding-your-on-screen-double-chin-11590069979.
4. Minda Zetlin, "Remote Employees Face a Greater Risk of Burnout. Here's How You Can Help," *Inc.*, June 8, 2020, https://www.inc.com/minda-zetlin/remote-work-employees-burnout-zillow-founder-rich-barton.html.
5. Amy Cuddy, "Your Body Language May Shape Who You Are," filmed June 2012 in Edinburgh Scotland, TedGlobal video, 20:46, https://www.ted.com/talks/amy_cuddy_your_body_language_may_shape_who_you_are.
6. Paul Dennison & Gail Dennison, *Brain Gym* (USA: Edu Kinesthetics, 1992).
7. Alison Wood Brooks, "Get Excited: Reappraising Pre-Performance Anxiety as Excitement.," *Journal of Experimental*

Psychology 143, no. 3 (2014): 1144–58, https://doi.org/10.1037/a0035325.

8. Julia Sklar, "'Zoom Fatigue' Is Taxing the Brain. Here's Why That Happens.," *National Geographic*, April 24, 2020, https://www.nationalgeographic.com/science/2020/04/coronavirus-zoom-fatigue-is-taxing-the-brain-here-is-why-that-happens/.

9. Chip Cutter, "Even the CEO of Zoom Says He Has Zoom Fatigue," *Wall Street Journal*, May 4, 2015, https://www.wsj.com/articles/even-the-ceo-of-zoom-says-he-has-zoom-fatigue-11620151459.

10. Sklar, "'Zoom Fatigue.'"

11. Sklar, "'Zoom Fatigue.'"

12. Sklar, "'Zoom Fatigue.'"

13. Dr. Mila Ioussifova, personal communication, for more information on Dr. Ioussifova see https://www.southwaterfronteyecare.com/.

Chapter 6 Words to LOSE | Words to USE

1. After I began to notice words that were overused or misused in conversations and the culture at large, I read the book Playing Big by Tara Mohr. Her work (and that of others) influenced me to create the Confidence Project's module called Words to USE and Words to LOSE. My clients tell me this module is one of the most impactful for growing and supporting their confidence. Tara Mohr, Playing Big: Practical Wisdom for Women Who Want to Speak Up, Create, and Lead, Reprint edition (New York: Avery, 2015).

2. For more about Linda Brice, language, and word choice see her website Transformational Voice at https://www.transformationalvoice.com/.

3. Patricia Fripp, "About the Training," Fripp VT, accessed March 7, 2022, https://www.frippvt.com/

4. IMDb, "Owen Wilson-'Wow' Supercut," YouTube video, 00:58, July 12, 2020, https://www.youtube.com/watch?v=uOXuc3pV8mk.

5. George Lakoff, "Hedges: A Study in Meaning Criteria and the Logic of Fuzzy Concepts," *Journal of Philosophical Logic 2*, no. 4 (1973): 458–508. https://www.jstor.org/stable/30226076.

6. Seth Godin, "Luck Is not a Strategy," *Seth's Blog* (blog), June 29, 2021, https://seths.blog/2021/06/luck-is-not-a-strategy/.

7. Lauren McGoodwin, "Real Talk on Every Professional Topic We Can Imagine," Career Contessa, accessed March 7, 2022, https://www.careercontessa.com/about/.

8. Shonda Rhimes, *Year of Yes: How to Dance it Out, Stand in the Sun and Be Your Own Person* (New York: Simon & Schuster, 2015).

9. Dictionary.com, s.v. "cocky," accessed April 18, 2022, https://www.dictionary.com/browse/cocky.

10. Dictionary.com, s.v. "confident," accessed April 18, 2022, https://www.dictionary.com/browse/confident.

11. Michael Barbaro, interview with Ben Casselman, "Did Democrats Make Inflation Worse?" *The Daily*, audio podcast, February 1, 2022, https://www.nytimes.com/2022/02/01/podcasts/the-daily/inflation-pandemic-biden-economy.html.

12. L. Carol Ritchie, "'TBH' and 'Dad Bod' Are Among Merriam Webster's 455 New Words," *NPR*, October 28, 2021, https://www.npr.org/2021/10/28/1050034580/tbh-and-dad-bod-are-among-merriam-websters-455-newest-words-because-language.

13. "How Women Undermine Themselves with Words," Goop, April 14, 2015, https://goop.com/wellness/career-money/how-women-undermine-themselves-with-words/.

14. John Herrman "The Rise and Fall of 'Zuck Talk,'" *New York Times*, September 1, 2021, https://www.nytimes.com/2021/09/01/style/right-so-speech.html.

15. Kimberly Joki, "Ending a Sentence with a Preposition: It's Ok and It's Not," *Grammarly* (blog), September 3, 2014, https://www.grammarly.com/blog/youve-been-lied-to-heres-why-you-absolutely-can-end-a-sentence-with-a-preposition/.

16. Joki, "Ending a Sentence."

17. Anne Marie Chaker, "We're Cursing More. Blame the #%$ Pandemic." *Wall Street Journal*," December 20, 2021, https://www.wsj.com/articles/were-cursing-more-blame-the-pandemic-11640008801.

18. Chaker, "We're Cursing More."

Chapter 7 The New Apology

1. John B. Waterhouse, *The Sorry Syndrome: How to Learn from Missteps Without Apologizing* (Los Angeles: Park Point Press, 2017).

2. "Just Not Sorry—the Chrome Extension," Chrome Web Store, accessed March 8, 2022, https://chrome.google.com/webstore/detail/just-not-sorry-the-chrome/fmegmibednnlgojepmidhlhpjbppmlci.

3. James R. Hagerty, "Jim Mills Built Medline Industries into a Giant of Medical Supplies," *Wall Street Journal*, July 19, 2019, https://www.wsj.com/articles/jim-mills-built-medline-industries-into-a-giant-of-medical-supplies-11563546600.

4. Juliet Eilperin, "White House Women Want to Be in the Room Where It Happens," *Washington Post*, September 13, 2016, https://www.washingtonpost.com/news/powerpost/wp/2016/09/13/white-house-women-are-now-in-the-room-where-it-happens/.

5. Linda Brice, personal communication, for more information on Linda Brice and the importance of voice see the website *Transformational Voice* at https://www.transformationalvoice.com/.

6. Linda Brice, *Transformational Voice*.

Chapter 8 Own Your Name + Honor Others

1. Terry Gross, "'Fresh Air' Remembers Civil Rights Leader Rep. John Lewis," recorded 2009, accessed November 11, 2020, https://www.npr.org/2020/07/20/892988572/fresh-air-remembers-civil-rights-leader-rep-john-lewis.

2. Dennis P. Carmody and Michael Lewis, "Brain Activation When Hearing One's Own and Others' Names," *Brain Research* 1116, no. 1 (October 20, 2006): 153–58, https://doi.org/10.1016/j.brainres.2006.07.121.
3. "Home," NameCoach, accessed June 20, 2022, https://cloud.name-coach.com/.

Chapter 9 The New Networking

1. "Social Distancing Wristband Kits," Elation Factory, accessed March 6, 2022, https://elationfactory.com/collections/social-distancing-wristband-kits-collection.
2. Jennifer Levitz, "New Pandemic Era Accessory: A Bracelet That Signals Your Boundaries," *Wall Street Journal*, June 7, 2021, https://www.wsj.com/articles/new-pandemic-era-accessory-a-bracelet-that-signals-your-boundaries-11623076293.
3. Dara Prant, "Must Read: Oprah Covers 'WSJ Magazine's' March Fashion Issue, Tom Ford on His Upcoming Shows," Fashionista, February 6, 2018, https://fashionista.com/2018/02/oprah-wsj-magazine-march-2018.
4. Charlotte Cowles, "Tap LinkedIn for Career Opportunities," *New York Times*, October 31, 2020, https://www.nytimes.com/2020/10/31/at-home/linkedin-career-opportunities.html.
5. Joseph McCormack, *Brief: Make a Bigger Impact by Saying Less* (Hoboken, NJ: John Wiley & Sons, 2014).
6. Suzanne Oliver, How to Build Stronger Relationships with Colleagues in the Zoom Era, *Wall Street Journal*, November 26, 2021, https://www.wsj.com/articles/build-stronger-relationships-on-zoom-11637608490.
7. Laura Collins-Hughes, "Cherished Words from Sondheim, Theater's Encourager-in-Chief," New York Times, December 1, 2021, https://www.nytimes.com/2021/12/01/theater/stephen-sondheim-mentor-notes.html

Chapter 10 Confident Conversations

1. "Meet Sherri," Sherri Fitts, accessed March 7, 2022, https://sherifitts.com/meet-sheri/.

2. Mel Robbins, *The 5 Second Rule: Transform Your Life, Work, and Confidence with Everyday Courage* (USA: Savio Republic, 2017).

3. Benjamin Fearnow, "The Best Quotes by Larry King: I Never Learned Anything While I Was Talking," Newsweek, January 23, 2021, https://www.newsweek.com/best-quotes-larry-king-i-never-learned-anything-while-i-was-talking-1563928.

Chapter 11 The New Goodbye

1. Elisabeth Perlman, "This Watch Will Tell You When You're Being Boring," Verdict, anuFebruary 7, 2017, https://www.verdict.co.uk/watch-will-tell-youre-boring/.

Chapter 12 The Hybrid Highway

1. Heidi Grant and Tal Goldhamer, "Our Brains Were Not Built for This Much Uncertainty," *Harvard Business Review*, September 22, 2021, https://hbr.org/2021/09/our-brains-were-not-built-for-this-much-uncertainty.

2. Grant and Goldhamer, "Our Brains."

3. Grant and Goldhamer, "Our Brains."

4. Microsoft, "The Next Great Disruption Is Hybrid Work—Are We Ready?" March 22, 2021, https://www.microsoft.com/en-us/worklab/work-trend-index/hybrid-work.

5. Holger Reisinger and Dane Fetterer, "Forget Flexibility. Your Employees Want Autonomy." *Harvard Business Review*, October 29, 2021, https://hbr.org/2021/10/forget-flexibility-your-employees-want-autonomy.

6. Harry Klaff, see https://www.linkedin.com/in/harry-klaff/.

7. Avison Young, for more information about Avison Young see https://www.avisonyoung.us/en-US/.

8. Anna Jones, "How to Ask Your Boss for a Hybrid-Working Set Up," BBC, August 18, 2021, https://www.bbc.com/worklife/

article/20210817-how-to-ask-your-boss-for-a-hybrid-working-set-up.

9. Jones, "How to Ask Your Boss."
10. Jones, "How to Ask Your Boss."
11. Julia Wuench, "How to Ask Your Boss to Work From Home Permanently, *Forbes*, April 26, 2021, https://www.forbes.com/sites/juliawuench/2021/04/26/how-to-ask-your-boss-to-work-from-home-permanently/?sh=4aa3ece8ba2d
12. Wuench, "How to Ask Your Boss to Work From Home."
13. Jones, "How to Ask Your Boss for a Hybrid-Working Set-Up."
14. Carol S. Dweck, *Mindset: The New Psychology of Success* (New York: Ballantine Books, 2008).
15. C. S. Dweck and E. L. Leggett, "A Social-Cognitive Approach to Motivation and Personality," *Psychological Review* 95, no. 2 (1988): 256-273.
16. Bobby Herrera, *The Gift of Struggle: Life Changing Lessons about Leading* (Bard Press, 2019).
17. Michael Thompson, "The 8 Traits of Highly Confident People," Ladders, May 12, 2020, https://www.theladders.com/career-advice/the-8-traits-of-highly-confident-people.
18. Thompson, "The 8 Traits."
19. Felix Richter, "The Great Resignation Record: How Many Americans Left Their Jobs in November 2021?" World Economic Forum, January 18, 2022, https://www.weforum.org/agenda/2022/01/the-great-resignation-in-numbers-record/.
20. Aimee Picchi, "Job Openings Near Record High, with 11 Million Vacancies," CBS News, December 8, 2021, https://www.cbsnews.com/news/job-openings-11-million-near-record/
21. Arindrajit Dube (@arindube), "The Great Reshuffling continues, as workers leave bad jobs for better ones…, Twitter, March 9, 2022, https://twitter.com/arindube/status/1501605259117928451

忙

忙

自勺 adj   object
地   adv   verb
得

Made in the USA
Columbia, SC
05 October 2022